ONE THING

A GOSPEL-CENTERED LIFE ON MISSION

SMALL-GROUP STUDY

BEN HARRELL

IMB
Richmond, VA

Printed in the United States of America
19 18 17 16 15   1 2 3 4 5

ISBN-13: 978-0-9855403-4-0 (softcover)
ISBN-13: 978-0-9855403-5-7 (eBook)

Our mission is evangelizing, discipling and planting reproducing churches among all peoples in fulfillment of the Great Commission. Our vision is a multitude from every language, people, tribe and nation knowing and worshipping our Lord Jesus Christ. The *Baptist Faith and Message 2000* is our doctrinal guideline.

Editor: Mary Jane Welch
Cover and Illustrations: Betsy Lance

imb.org

CONTENTS

THE AUTHOR

My name is Ben, I'm from Tennessee, and I serve as a church planter and trainer with IMB. I have primarily been involved in providing access to the gospel to one of the least reached people groups in Asia. As a part of that effort, I've had the opportunity to train underground churches, nationally and within unreached people groups, to further reach their own people and other unreached people groups with the gospel.

I studied accounting and finance at the University of Tennessee and theology and intercultural leadership at The Southern Baptist Theological Seminary. Before moving overseas, I worked as a credit analyst. When my wife and I applied for overseas service with IMB we asked on our application form to be sent to the hardest places physically, spiritually, and emotionally—and we've certainly experienced some of each along the way.

I live in Asia with my wife and two children and value doing ministry as a family. I enjoy studying, working out, exploring new places, meeting new people, and trying new foods. The things I miss most about home, besides family, are Southern barbeque and hiking in the Smokies. Above all, I have a passion for God and making Him known among all peoples.

INTRODUCTION

The mission of the church is to make disciples. Any mission, especially one of this magnitude, requires that we understand what is expected and where we are headed. It's certainly a good idea to understand the people and places where we serve and biblically define the mission. But I also want to stress that an important part of understanding this mission is examining the type of people we should be.

I pray that this study provides an opportunity for you to go deeper in the Word to answer two questions:

WHAT DOES IT MEAN TO BE A DISCIPLE OF JESUS?

HOW DO WE MAKE DISCIPLES OF JESUS?

If God has taught my wife and me any one thing in our journey—through sharing the gospel and training young churches, through facing trials and transitions, through searching and studying—it has been a growing depth in what it means to surrender to Him. Others have said that the one thing we need is to know God, to delight in God, to desire God, to worship God, to experience God, to follow God, or to center everything on the gospel. In my mind, these are all different ways of expressing the same thing. From early in my walk with Christ, the way I have connected with this is through what Jesus pointed out to Martha and the rich ruler and through the examples of David and Paul.[1] Jesus told Martha that "one thing is necessary" (Luke 10:42). He told the rich ruler, "One thing you still lack. Sell all that you have and distribute to the poor, and you will have treasure in heaven; and come, follow me" (Luke 18:22). David wrote, "One thing have I asked of the Lord, that will I seek after: that I may dwell in the house of the Lord all the days of my life, to gaze upon the beauty of the Lord and to inquire in his temple" (Psalm 27:4).

To me, the fullest description of what this one thing looks like is found in Paul's example. Paul wrote, "Indeed, I count everything as loss because of the surpassing worth of knowing Christ Jesus my Lord" (Philippians 3:8a). Paul continued by, I think groaningly, expressing his willingness to face any and every challenge in that pursuit:

> For his sake I have suffered the loss of all things and count them as rubbish, in order that I may gain Christ and be found in him, not having a righteousness of my own that comes from the law, but that which comes through faith in Christ, the righteousness from God that depends on faith—that I may know him and the power of his resurrection, and may share his sufferings, becoming like him in his death, that by any means possible I may attain the resurrection from the dead (Philippians 3:8b-11).

And in what he writes next, he tells us how he foremost focused his efforts. "One thing I do: forgetting what lies behind and straining forward to what lies ahead, I press on toward the goal for the prize of the upward call of God in Christ Jesus" (Philippians 3:13b-14). We then read that he shared his testimony here for the purpose of calling the Philippians, and us, to also live this way:

> Brothers, join in imitating me, and keep your eyes on those who walk according to the example you have in us. For many, of whom I have often told you and now tell you even with tears, walk as enemies of the cross of Christ (Philippians 3:17-18).

God's desire is for you to increasingly grow to delight in Him and become like His Son (Romans 8:29). When we remain connected to the Son, the fruit is growth both as a disciple and as a disciple who makes disciples—apart from Him we can do nothing (John 15:4-17). So this one thing must be what drives us and what all our activities stem from, as J.C. Ryle wrote:

> A zealous man in religion is pre-eminently a man of one thing. It is not enough to say that he is earnest, hearty, uncompromising, thorough-going, wholehearted, fervent in spirit. He sees one thing, he cares for one thing, he lives for one thing, he is swallowed-up in one thing—and that one thing is to please God.
>
> Whether he lives—or whether he dies;
> whether he has health—or whether he has sickness;
> whether he is rich—or whether he is poor;
> whether he pleases man—or whether he gives offence;
> whether he is thought wise—or whether he is thought foolish;
> whether he gets blame—or whether he gets praise;
> whether he gets honor, or whether he gets shame
> —for all this the zealous man cares nothing at all. He burns for one thing—and that one thing is to please God, and to advance God's glory. If he is consumed in the very burning—he is content. He feels that, like a lamp, he is made to burn, and if consumed in burning—he has but done the work for which God appointed him.[2]

By the grace of God and indwelling work of His Spirit, may this be true of each of us.

HOW TO USE THIS STUDY

As you step out on mission, I encourage you to join others in worship, the Word, and prayer to obey all that Jesus commanded. This "Small-Group Study" version of *One Thing* was formatted for discipleship groups or teams preparing for volunteer projects.[1] Leaders should prepare for each week's meeting using the complete *One Thing: A Gospel-Centered Life on Mission*. The complete version includes all nine sessions, an Answer Key, a Facilitator Guide with other suggested formats, and additional content that has been abridged from this version.

Weekly Meetings

I recommend meeting weekly for about two hours to review the material through accountability, worship, Bible study, and prayer. Try to provide flexibility in your time together, and be willing to change and adapt as needed. Aim to provide sufficient time for everyone to respond and for the Holy Spirit to guide your group. At the same time, keep an eye on the clock so as to not get unnecessarily sidetracked. Take each third seriously (start, study, and surrender)—these are the critical components that create a culture of discipleship.

Steps to Prepare

1. **Pray.** Pray for each other prior to, during, and after this study. Pray for the people and places you will be going to serve.

2. **Read the sessions.** Study each session in advance and answer the questions. Encourage each other to really dig into the passages presented in each session and take time to read and consider the content and suggestions.

3. **Adapt the material.** As you study the material, make notes on how the concepts may specifically play out and apply to your context.

4. **Add personal stories.** Think of personal stories that may relate to each session before your weekly meeting. Try to be concise when you share your stories with the group so as to not unnecessarily take too much time from the Bible study.

5. **Study the Bible passages.** Set aside some extra time in advance to read the passages in each session and study them for yourself—work to internalize the portions of Scripture being studied.

6. **Plan songs for worship.** Assign someone each week to select the worship songs that you will sing during worship time. If you have musicians in your group, you may want to ask them if they would like to help lead the singing. If no one in your group is musically inclined, plan music that you can sing a cappella or download mp3s or videos to follow. Prepare and provide the lyrics, whether from a hymnal, a printed sheet, or on a projector.

7. **Communicate with your field partner(s).** Whether you are preparing for a short-term or mid-term project, or a long-term assignment, ask questions for the overseas church planters you will be working with. They are a critical resource of the strategic, logistical, and security situations in the area where you will serve. Follow their lead and recommendations.

Plans

The "Your Plan" pages are designed for developing long-term strategies and accountability. As you may be coming alongside an existing church-planting team, all questions may not apply but may be helpful in understanding the overall strategy for engaging the people group or city. As you go through the worksheets, adapt questions as necessary for your context.

If you've been burdened for a particular need or group of people, then take the time to really explore what the Father is asking you to do. Examine the Word. Research the details. Seek wise counsel. Ask, pray, and trust the Spirit to guide. As your burdens become clearer, write them down, both when starting a new journey and when continuing on one.

Join with other believers and put yourself in a position to maximize your ability to be obedient.

I pray that as you join others in the study of God's Word that you gain confidence and feel empowered to boldly step out in faith. I pray that you are given new reasons to praise the Lord every day and that whether you are in times of trouble or peace, His name be glorified in and through your life.

> Oh sing to the LORD a new song;
> sing to the LORD, all the earth!
> Sing to the LORD, bless his name;
> tell of his salvation from day to day.
> Declare his glory among the nations (Psalm 96:1-3).

BE A DISCIPLE

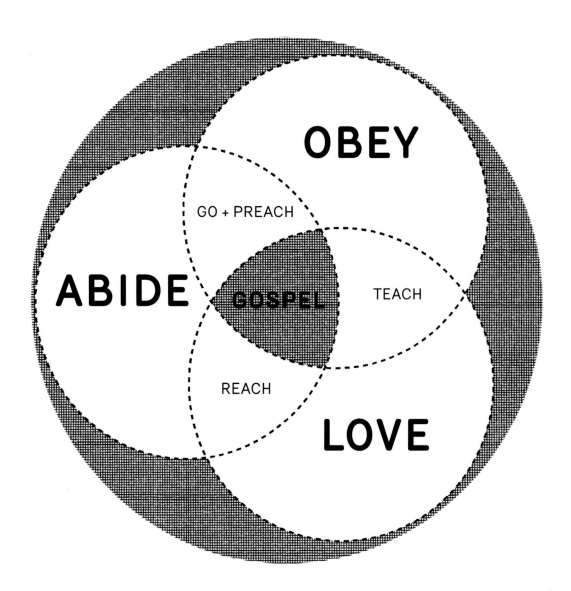

Indeed, I count everything as loss because of the surpassing worth of knowing Christ Jesus my Lord. For his sake I have suffered the loss of all things and count them as rubbish, in order that I may gain Christ PHILIPPIANS 3:8.

Consider the great missionary Paul. The overall emphasis of his letters wasn't on missions. Rather, the focus was on pointing people to Jesus—his primary passion was knowing Jesus. In our zeal for *making* disciples, we must not take *being* a disciple for granted. This is at the core of why we go on mission. The yearning felt within us to take the gospel to the lost is first met by going to the gospel ourselves. We must focus on this one thing. We must ask ourselves if we are fully surrendered to God. Have you given over everything that hinders you and every sin that entangles you? Are you striving to obey all that Jesus commanded? Are you loving people along the way?

In this section we are going to ask what it means to be a disciple. Just before Jesus' arrest the night of the Passover supper in the upper room, He provided His apostles with clear direction for the days ahead. It was an amazing conversation—a convocation speech, if you will—that set the stage for the mission they were about to set out on. We are going to examine how a gospel-centered life is a life fully surrendered to God. It's a life that follows the leading of His Spirit. And it's a life that includes certain responsibilities, which we are going to study by examining what Jesus focused the apostles' attention on: to abide in Him, to obey His commands, and to love one another.

GOSPEL-CENTERED LIFE
A disciple of Jesus is forgiven of his or her sins and surrendered to God: "And he touched my mouth and said: 'Behold, this has touched your lips; your guilt is taken away, and your sin atoned for.' And I heard the voice of the Lord saying, 'Whom shall I send, and who will go for us?' Then I said, 'Here I am! Send me'" (Isaiah 6:7-8).
    gospel-centered *adj.* everything focused on Jesus and what He did

ABIDE
A disciple of Jesus abides in Him: "I am the vine; you are the branches. Whoever abides in me and I in him, he it is that bears much fruit, for apart from me you can do nothing" (John 15:5).
    abide *v.* to remain connected and committed to Jesus

OBEY
A disciple of Jesus obeys: "If you keep my commandments, you will abide in my love, just as I have kept my Father's commandments and abide in his love" (John 15:10, ESV).
    obey *v.* to follow the teaching of the Word and guidance of the Spirit

LOVE
A disciple of Jesus loves: "This is my commandment, that you love one another as I have loved you" (John 15:12).
    love *v.* to genuinely express interest, care, and honor

ALTAR AT A FRIEND'S HOME.

GOSPEL-CENTERED LIFE

For God gave us a spirit not of fear but of power and love and self-control. Therefore do not be ashamed of the testimony about our Lord, nor of me his prisoner, but share in suffering for the gospel by the power of God, who saved us and called us to a holy calling, not because of our works but because of his own purpose and grace.
2 TIMOTHY 1:7-9A

In this session, we will explore the necessity of absolute surrender. We will study the Word to learn about living a gospel-centered life, depending on the Spirit and seeking God in prayer. Here's the main idea:

The gospel is foundational to every aspect of our life and mission—we must stay focused on Jesus as the source for all that we are and all that we do.

SESSION OUTLINE
- Absolute Surrender
- Gospel-Centered Life
  - Abide
  - Obey
  - Love
- The Helper
- Prayer
  - Elijah
  - Epaphras
  - Paul

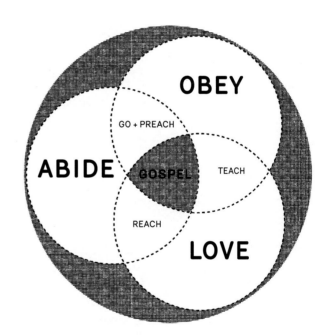

START

Welcome to your first One Thing small-group meeting.

Welcome
Have everyone introduce themselves and share why they joined this study.

Start *One Thing*
Use the questions below to start your discussion of *One Thing*.

What does it mean to be a disciple of Jesus?

How do we make disciples?

What does being a disciple and making disciples currently look like for you, your church, and the ministries you are involved in? What should it look like?

What do you feel burdened for? What people group(s), area(s), and/or need(s) come to your attention over and over again? In prayer and trusting the Spirit to work, what do you hope to see happen?

Worship + Parable Study[1]
Spend some time worshipping God together in song.

Read Matthew 18:21-35, "The Unforgiving Servant."

What is the main message of this parable?

What does the parable tell us about how the kingdom grows?

What is our part?

What should we expect and how should you respond?

STUDY

The places of worship for two major religions, plus a seemingly endless number of small animistic temples, dotted the countryside of our first overseas assignment. The mountains above the villages typically had sacrificial altars and prayer flags honoring the gods that the local tribes believed would bring them blessing or hardship. The first thing you saw as you entered their dirt-brick homes was an altar to a god. Above the doorway of their kitchen was yet another. Nearly everywhere you turned there was an inescapable and undivided expression of culture and religion. In our next assignment, the diversity of religions, idols, gods, and places of worship may have been even more pronounced. As we live in these places, our hearts are daily stirred for these people and broken before God.

Our prayer is that the love, knowledge, and experience of the true God will saturate every aspect of our lives and one day theirs as well. But, as we pursue this, it leads me to regularly ask how my knowledge about God is affecting me. This is not simply a question of understanding what the words or experiences mean; rather it's a question that probes deeply into how my life is being transformed. Does my life show evidence that I am fully surrendered to God?

Absolute Surrender[3]

Isaiah 6 paints a convicting picture of how a high view of God can and should transform us.[2] We know that Isaiah was a prophet of God, so we can assume he probably already knew a fair amount about God. But what happened when he had a rare, direct encounter with God?

Read Isaiah 6:1-4. Considering the scene in these verses, what can we know about God?

Isaiah 6:5. How did Isaiah respond in the presence of God?

Isaiah 6:6-7. What was the purpose of the coal? What was given to Isaiah?

Isaiah 6:8. What was Isaiah's response when asked, "Who will go?"

Isaiah 6:9-13. What was Isaiah being asked to do and what was he told to expect?

Isaiah was allowed a glimpse of the glory of God that man is ordinarily not allowed to see. That experience led him to brokenness and complete surrender to God's will. When he heard the voice of the Lord ask who would go, he likely didn't know what was coming. You see, he wasn't asked to be some kind of superstar leader or loved speaker. Far from it—he was asked to proclaim doom and judgment (Isaiah 6:9-12). This isn't some rosy little story about going on mission and following God because it's the cool thing to do. The application here is important: Isaiah was brought *in* to be sent *out*; he was convicted and cleansed, which brought him into the conversation and gave him his mission and the perseverance to carry it out.

This powerful story really stands on its own, but the experience of our first overseas assignment made this passage even more tangible for me. It was one of those places where it was far from easy to be a Christian. Large numbers of people weren't turning to follow Jesus.

I remember studying this passage with our local brothers and sisters shortly after a very destructive earthquake. When we read about how the the foundations of the thresholds shook in the presence of God, the high loss of life in those impoverished areas came to our minds. After that event, many contemplated the realities of eternity like never before. Priorities have a way of quickly coming into sharp focus during such serious and uncertain events. And so, even in the face of opposition and persecution, their overwhelming sense of God's presence and love compelled them to share with their families, their friends, and the strangers down the road.

God often uses circumstances to make us aware of His presence. If you were Isaiah, how would you respond to such a call? Would you go through with it? This kind of absolute surrender and complete dependence on God is something we all need. How can we do what we are called to do unless we humbly walk in awe of and submission to this all-powerful and praiseworthy God whose glory fills the whole earth?

Gospel-Centered Life
The eight sessions that follow stem out of the last conversation Jesus had with His disciples before His arrest—a conversation about both being a disciple and making disciples. He clearly defined and provided grounding for what His responsibility is and what we've been entrusted to do. We need to understand what falls to His responsibility—we need to trust Him in that. But we shouldn't be overly concerned about those things. That evening, Jesus focused the disciples' attention on three actions: to abide in Him, to obey His commands, and to love one another. What He said was simple but also very profound. It was a conversation about together continuing the mission He gave us—a mission that requires complete dependence on Him and His Spirit.

The gospel is foundational to every aspect of our life and mission. We must keep our focus on Jesus, "the founder and perfecter of our faith," for all that we are and all that we do (Hebrews 12:2). It's out of a love-driven, abiding relationship with Him that we obey. And it's from Him that convictions arise within us to point each new generation of disciples to live for Christ.

We will use the following diagram as a guide to dig deeper in the Word and examine what a gospel-centered life is all about. As the actions of abiding, obeying, and loving come together, we go from being a disciple to making disciples, which is the focus of the next section. For now, let's just establish a place to start as we begin looking at how this might impact our life and our mission.

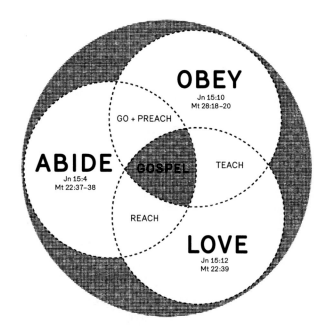

Abide

Abide is the first circle we will look at. Abiding has to do with our identity and everything about us remaining connected and committed to Jesus. But what does abiding look like? Jesus was once asked what the greatest or most important commandment was. As a starting point, examine the first part of His response, along with what He said in John 15.

Read Matthew 22:37-38. What does abiding in Jesus look like?

Read John 15:4-6. When should you abide in Jesus?

We must go from knowing who God is to surrendering to who God is, which includes relinquishing everything and solely living for God. We must seek to recognize and humbly acknowledge our own inadequacies, and we must strive to live spiritually disciplined and holy lives. And so, in life and on mission, this ongoing pursuit must remain our core priority.

Obey
Next, let's look at obedience by examining John 14 and 15 together with the Great Commission.

Matthew 28:18-20. What are we to obey?

Read John 14:15, 24; John 15:9-10. Why do we obey?

It's critical that our obedience stems out of love in order for it to be sustainable. We love because He first loved us (1 John 4:19). It's that love that enables us to abide. It's because of that love that we are driven to obey Him. It takes a lot of time and a lot of maturity to get there, but that's what we are always aiming for. By faith we take radical steps of obedience. And radical steps of obedience provide new opportunities for our faith to be strengthened.

Love
Finally, think about what love looks like by considering what Jesus said in John 13 and 15, along with the second part of His response to being questioned about the greatest commandment.

Read Matthew 22:39; John 13:34-35; 15:12-14. Who should we love? How should we love?

The love of Christ should compel us to make every effort to genuinely care for the people around us and around the world. Participating with other believers in community and on mission offers us the opportunity to more authentically grow in Christ and reach others with the gospel. We need to remember that we each bring different experiences, personalities, convictions, and skill sets to the table. We should strive to work in a spirit of unity so that as one we may glorify God.

The Helper

Jesus said, "Whoever believes in me will also do the works that I do; and greater works than these will he do" (John 14:12). (Greater works than Jesus? For whoever believes in Him? Really?!) In many ways this is an impossible task. Jesus knew this. So that night before His arrest, He promised the apostles a Helper, the Holy Spirit, who would be with them forever. What seemed impossible was made possible through Him. This was a promise not only for the apostles but also for all who would believe. Jesus continued, "By this my Father is glorified, that you bear much fruit and so prove to be my disciples" (John 15:8). The Holy Spirit helped them on their mission and is promised to help us as we continue it.

Read John 7:37-39. When Jesus describes the Holy Spirit as "rivers of living water," what comes to mind?

Read John 14:15-31; 15:26-16:15. How is the Holy Spirit promised to help?

I want to be one of the fruit-bearing believers that Jesus spoke about, and I believe that, because we are followers of Jesus, our passion and love for Him should be evident in our lives. We should be passionate and persuasive about the gospel. At the same time, we've got to remember that it's really not about you or me persuading anyone—only the Spirit convicts and only Jesus saves. In order to be effective in anything we do, we must be Spirit-filled and Spirit-led. The Spirit reminds us of the truths He has taught us, He gives us peace, and He guides us. He knows the message that each person needs to hear. The promise and presence of the Holy Spirit's help give great comfort and confidence that this mission really is possible.

As Jesus departed from His earthly ministry, He left us with these words, "You will receive power when the Holy Spirit has come upon you, and you will be my witnesses in Jerusalem and in all Judea and Samaria, and to the ends of the earth" (Acts 1:8). Over the next 10 days,

120 followers of Jesus gathered in an upper room in Jerusalem. They prayed and waited. Then, on the day of the Jewish feast of Pentecost, the Spirit came down and filled them. The gospel was preached boldly and, as a sign of the Spirit and the power of God, many who made the pilgrimage from distant places to attend the feast heard the Word in their own language. In all, 3,000 were rescued into God's kingdom that day, and the numbers continued to increase day by day.[4]

Prayer

On the night of His arrest, Jesus provided His disciples with direction and encouragement for the days ahead. Woven throughout the conversation was also a message on prayer.[5] It makes sense that He would instruct them about prayer, but what He says is almost shocking— "whatever you ask in my name, this I will do" (John 14:13). He later closed in prayer for His disciples, and they headed out to the garden where He would be arrested. Jesus' statements on prayer are often ignored or relegated to only certain aspects of our lives. But how should we apply what He said?

Read John 14:12-14; 15:7. What did Jesus say about our requests?

What are you asking Him for? What can you ask Him for?

Even though what Jesus said about prayer can be difficult to understand or believe, it is no less true. James helps to bring balance, as we might otherwise respond incorrectly. On the one hand, he reminds us of our need to pray. "You do not have, because you do not ask" (James 4:2c). On the other hand, he exhorts us not to be selfish in our prayers. "You ask and do not receive, because you ask wrongly, to spend it on your own passions" (James 4:3).[6] It might be helpful to look at a few examples: Elijah, Epaphras, and Paul. These are three men whose prayer journeys were recorded as models for us.

Elijah
Read James 5:17-18 (see also 1 Kings 17-18). Where was Elijah's confidence? Can you pray like Elijah?

Epaphras

Read Colossians 1:3-8; 4:12. What did Epaphras want for the believers in Colossae? How did he pray for them?

Paul

Paul is well-known as the great New Testament missionary, but he also was a man of prayer. The verses to study are many, so here I will provide just an overview. (If you'd like to do this study on your own, the references have been provided in the endnotes for this chapter.[7])

Throughout the book of Acts and in his letters, Paul is praying. He spoke about the need to be steadfast, watchful, constant, and unceasing in prayer. He taught us to pray with both our spirit and our mind. When we don't know what to pray, he told us that the Spirit will help and intercede for us. He taught us to pray everywhere and for everyone. And he exhorted us to not be anxious, angry, or quarrelsome. Instead, we should pray, intercede for others, and be thankful.

Paul modeled what he taught. Everywhere he went he prayed—after his conversion, throughout his missionary journeys, and in prison. In anticipation of the places he would go and in follow-up to the places he had been, he prayed for believers and the lost. On his second missionary journey, around midnight and in prison, he and Silas prayed and sang hymns to God. He prayed for the spreading of the gospel, for the salvation of the lost, and for the healing of the sick. Paul prayed for the growth of disciples and for God to be glorified through them. He prayed for believers to grow and for unity to be restored. He prayed as he committed elders to the Lord, and he asked the churches to pray for him and for his ministry. And even though there were often issues that required confrontation, Paul was thankful for those churches in his prayers. His life was marked by a constant yearning for God and ceaseless prayer.

Read Ephesians 3:14-21; Colossians 1:9-14; 2 Thessalonians 1:11-12. How should you pray as you make disciples? What should you pray for as you make disciples?

You should regularly evaluate your prayer life. Do you trust God to provide what you need and answer your prayers? What are you asking God for?

No matter where you live and what your days look like, you have the choice each day to depend on yourself, to live safely, and to try to control your life. Or you can live as you were created to live—as a temple of the Holy Spirit of God, as a person dependent on Him, desperate for God the Spirit to show up and make a difference. When you begin living a life characterized by walking with the Spirit, that is when people will begin to look not to you but to our Father in heaven and give Him the praise.

—FRANCIS CHAN, *FORGOTTEN GOD*[8]

SURRENDER

Review
Use the following questions to briefly review the content of this week's study.

What did you learn in this week's study? What questions do you have?

What did you learn or what were you reminded of about God?

What did you learn about fully surrendering to His plans?

What did you learn about living a gospel-centered life?

What did you learn about the Holy Spirit?

What did you learn about prayer?

Response + Prayer
In groups of two or three, discuss the following questions.

How should your knowledge of God transform how you live?

How can you grow to become more faithfully constant, steadfast, and watchful in prayer?

What did you take away from this week's study? What will you do in response?

What prayer requests do you have?

How can we pray for our community?

How can we pray for the people we are going to serve?

Spend some time praying together.

YOUR PLAN: DEFINE YOUR VISION

WHERE ARE YOU AT?

What are you burdened about? What people group(s), area(s), and/or need(s) come to your attention over and over again?

WHERE ARE YOU GOING?

Prayerfully trusting the Spirit to work, what do you hope to see happen? Brainstorm and dream about what it is going to look like when you are done.

Best case scenario: What do you hope to see happen within five years? What do you hope to see this year?

Think and pray over your responses above. Write a statement that captures your vision.

THE BIBLE I CARRIED WHILE WRITING.

ABIDE

Abide in me, and I in you. As the branch cannot bear fruit by itself, unless it abides in the vine, neither can you, unless you abide in me. JOHN 15:4

You shall love the Lord your God with all your heart and with all your soul and with all your mind. This is the great and first commandment. MATTHEW 22:37-38

In this session, we will explore what it means to abide in Jesus. I think most of us who have been in church for a while have a general idea of what "abiding in Christ" means. But abide isn't a word we commonly use or hear. We will examine how the Bible defines this term and honestly ask if we exemplify that. Here's the main idea:

We must go from knowing who God is to surrendering to who God is, which includes relinquishing everything and living solely for God. We must seek to recognize and humbly acknowledge our own inadequacies, and we must strive to live spiritually disciplined and holy lives.

SESSION OUTLINE
- Abiding in Jesus
- Abiding in His Word

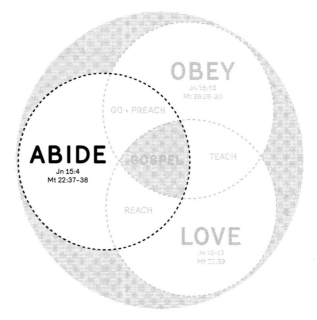

START

Welcome to this week's small-group meeting.

How are you?

How are you doing? How are we doing?

What has God been teaching you?

How have you obeyed what we discussed last week?

Did you share the gospel with anyone this week? How did it go?

Worship + Parable Study

Spend some time worshipping God together in song.

Read Matthew 13:44-46, "The Treasure and the Pearl."

What is the main message of these parables?

What do these parables tell us about how the kingdom grows?

What is our part?

What should we expect and how should you respond?

STUDY

Having just dropped the first piece of luggage by the door, I was making my way down the steps to my in-laws' basement as my phone rang. My doctor on the other end said, "I just received a report back. What is your housing situation?" Then at the end of a five-month assignment in the United States, we were scheduled to return overseas in less than 24 hours. He continued, "I'm going to need you to set up an appointment with a specialist as soon as you can." He had been doing some monitoring after a few levels that concerned him showed up in reports 10 months earlier. He had eliminated a number of potential causes, but was alarmed by this recent report. I asked when we would be able to return, and he said "I don't know. You need to get this followed up and taken care of before you can go back." My heart sank. I didn't know how to respond.

By God's grace there was a cancer specialist in our city who was able to see us within a couple of weeks. He verified the readings and reassured me that "in his gut" he thought I was fine—hardly the level of reassurance I was hoping for at the time! After another appointment, I was released with a requirement of regular follow-up over the next year. I had more tests done overseas a few months later at a leading regional hospital. There were still some strange readings but nothing diagnosable.

The following year, I had the cleanest bill of health in my adult life. It's not exactly clear what was going on—whether it was just my body reacting to too much stress or something more serious that I was healed from. But one thing is certain: the Father allowed me to take a glimpse at a dark part of my heart, break me, and make me desperate for Him.

Abiding in Jesus

To one group of believers Jesus said, "If you abide in my word, you are truly my disciples, and you will know the truth, and the truth will set you free" (John 8:31-32). And to His disciples He said, "I am the vine; you are the branches. Whoever abides in me and I in him, he it is that bears much fruit, for apart from me you can do nothing" (John 15:5). A life surrendered to Jesus looks different from an ordinary life. We should examine the difference between knowing Him and truly abiding in Him. The book of 1 John was written so that believers would have confidence in this life and would know what it means to abide in Jesus. The letter begins with the message of Jesus rescuing us out of darkness into light—a message of undeserved forgiveness and restored relationship that should affect every aspect of our lives.

Read the verses below. Describe what it looks like when we abide in Jesus.

1 John 2:6

1 John 2:9-10

1 John 2:14

1 John 2:15-17

1 John 2:24

1 John 2:27

1 John 2:28-29

1 John 3:9-10

1 John 3:17-18

1 John 3:23-24

1 John 4:12

1 John 4:13

1 John 4:15

The time between receiving the phone call from my doctor and going to my first appointment in a cancer institute was a dark time. I questioned God and the purpose of my time serving overseas up to that point. The emotions of a dangerous early labor and medical evacuation with the birth of our first child less than a year before were still fresh, and I questioned why He would now allow this to happen. I came close to questioning Him altogether. People would try to encourage me, "The Father has a plan; He'll use this for something good." But so often I just wanted to say, "Then you deal with this!" I didn't want to hear any of it.

Though I wish I could tell a different story, I didn't respond well to this situation. But I learned a lot in that season. The suffering only lasted for a little while, but it forced me to honestly examine myself. My desperation for God was deepened and my dependency on Him was strengthened. My desire to live fully surrendered in life and on mission was certainly intensified. It doesn't have to take difficult and even dire seasons to make us desperate for Him. He has given us all we need in His Son and graciously revealed all truth in His Word.

The book of 1 John is a picture of someone who abides in Jesus. Those who abide in Jesus walk as He walked and love as He loved. They are in the Word and stay focused on truth. They have confidence and experience the Spirit's presence in their lives. They are not distracted by the world or entangled in sin. It is helpful to know what an abiding life looks like. There are many more places we could reference to further study what it means to abide, such as the "fruit of the Spirit" passage—love, joy, peace, patience, kindness, goodness, faithfulness, gentleness, and self-control (Galatians 5:22-23). But don't concentrate on a spiritual checklist and neglect the one thing that's really needed. Spiritual fruit is produced from abiding in Him, and our obedience must grow out of a love for Him.

Abiding in His Word

In a short, simple parable, Jesus said, "The kingdom of heaven is like treasure hidden in a field, which a man found and covered up. Then in his joy he goes and sells all that he has and buys that field" (Matthew 13:44). Or consider what Job said, "I have treasured the words of his [God's] mouth more than my portion of food" (Job 23:12b). These are striking images of a man joyfully selling everything he has and another man treasuring God's words more than food. Are you focused on the Word of God and the kingdom of God in that way?

Paul explains his purpose in writing the letter to the church in Colossae "that their hearts may be encouraged, being knit together in love, to reach all the riches of full assurance of understanding and the knowledge of God's mystery, which is Christ, in whom are hidden all the treasures of wisdom and knowledge" (Colossians 2:2-3). In Jesus are hidden all the treasures of wisdom and knowledge. To be a person of deep understanding and wisdom requires a constant evaluation of your time and thoughts. This evaluation is not so much about your actions as it is about your attitudes and affections for God and His Word. You should examine not only what Jesus meant by abiding in Him but also what He meant by having His "words abide in you" (John 15:7). Do you really treasure His words? Are you desperate for Him?

There are many good guides out there for better understanding the Bible and how to study it. If they help and get you to spend more time in the Word, then by all means use them. Through the years, I have been blessed with numerous teachers and references that have helped me to grow in my study of the Bible. But more than the methods or processes, I'd have to say that I learned more from the increased time in the Word that those studies drove me to and from the passion that I saw in those mentors. With this in mind, let's now look at how we grow in the Word of God.

Read the passages below. In a word or phrase, describe how you grow in the Word of God.
Joshua 1:8; Psalm 1:2; 119:15-16, 97; Romans 7:22

Psalm 119:9

Psalm 119:10

Psalm 119:11; Deuteronomy 11:18

Deuteronomy 6:6-7

Deuteronomy 8:3; Matthew 4:4

Matthew 15:3-11

John 8:31-32; 15:7; Colossians 3:16

Acts 17:11

Ephesians 6:17

1 Timothy 4:13

2 Timothy 2:15

2 Timothy 3:16

James 1:22; Luke 6:46-49; 11:28

■ ▬ ■

There was in our company a godly worker who has much to do with training workers, and I asked him what he would say was the great need of the church, and the message that ought to be preached. He answered very quietly and determinedly: "Absolute surrender to God is the one thing."

—Andrew Murray, *Absolute Surrender*[1]

SURRENDER

Review
Use the following questions to briefly review the content of this week's study.

What does it mean to abide in Jesus?

What did you learn, or what were you reminded of, about your relationship with Jesus?

What makes the Bible unique?

What did you learn about abiding in His Word?

Response + Prayer
In groups of two or three, discuss the following questions.

What are you doing to spend time with Jesus and in His Word?

What spiritual disciplines do you need to put into practice?

What did you take away from this week's study? What will you do in response?

What prayer requests do you have?

How can we pray for our community?

How can we pray for the people we are going to serve?

Spend some time praying together.

YOUR PLAN: ABIDE

WHERE ARE YOU AT?

How are you spending time in the Bible?

How are you worshipping and praying?

What sins or attitudes are you currently struggling with? What is distracting you from staying focused on Jesus?

WHERE ARE YOU GOING?

What spiritual disciplines do you need to prioritize in order to continue to grow in godliness?

Think and pray over your responses above. Write a goal for how you will commit to abide in Jesus this year.

MED-EVAC FOR PRETERM LABOR WITH FIRST CHILD.

OBEY

If you keep my commandments, you will abide in my love, just as I have kept my Father's commandments and abide in his love. JOHN 15:10, ESV

Teaching them to observe all that I have commanded you. MATTHEW 28:20A, ESV

In this session, we will explore what it means to be an obedient follower of Jesus. What motivates a follower of Jesus to obey is radically different from what religion teaches. Our obedience stems out of love—it's Jesus' love working in us that compels us to obey. In this session, we are going to turn to the book of James to better understand how faith and obedience work together. We're also going to ask what is holding us back from fully surrendering to God's plan for our lives. Here's the main idea:

We are exposed, grow, and learn new things about ourselves and God through the journey of obedience. By faith we take radical steps of obedience. And radical steps of obedience provide new opportunities for our faith to be strengthened.

SESSION OUTLINE
- Obediently Following Jesus
- Trials and Persecution
- Healthy Living
  - Expectations
  - Examination

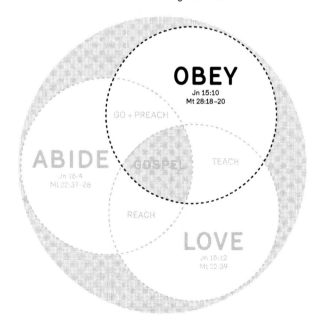

START

Welcome to this week's small-group meeting.

How are you?

How are you doing? How are we doing?

What has God been teaching you?

How have you obeyed what we discussed last week?

Did you share the gospel with anyone this week? How did it go?

Worship + Parable Study

Spend some time worshipping God together in song.

Read Matthew 21:33-46, "The Tenants."

What is the main message of this parable?

What does the parable tell us about how the kingdom grows?

What is our part?

What should we expect and how should you respond?

STUDY

We had secretly gathered a group of leaders from a little known people group to the city for a month-long workshop. The focus for the morning's devotion was Hebrews 12. "Consider him who endured for sinners such hostility against himself, so that you may not grow weary or fainthearted. In your struggle against sin you have not yet resisted to the point of shedding your blood" (Hebrews 12:3-4). During a time of discussion, my heart broke hearing many personal stories of opposition and persecution. Then, almost in unison, these brothers and sisters began to encourage one another to endure, as yet not one of them had yet suffered to the point of shedding their blood as Jesus had done for them!

They ended that time by laying hands on me and praying over the short trip that I was departing for immediately. This marked a very significant day for the ministry—this trip was to complete an effort to hand off the work in each population segment of our people group to national leaders. Over that year, we had an urgent and compelling sense that, for a season, the doors were open and we needed to push especially hard. The nationals I was with that day gained much confidence as many people were available and interested in hearing the gospel. Descending the mountain after visiting the last village, I had a real sense of gratitude and wonder over all that God had done and this work that He allowed us to be a part of.

And then we saw them: the group of armor-clad police officers stopped on the small mountain road we were traveling. Though I had traveled in the area hundreds of times before with no incidents, a new crackdown that we knew nothing about was in effect. We were brought down to a police station for an evening of questioning, which then turned into an investigation. It ended a couple of months later with me and my family expelled from the country.

Knowing this day could come at any time in such a location took little away from the emotional pain we experienced over the following months. Even still, I clearly remember, at 2 a.m. the night before we left, sitting on the floor of our quiet, empty apartment and shoving the last things that would fit into our limited luggage. Suddenly, this nearly tangible sense of joy and peace flooded over me. I felt immediately comforted and confident that we had done what He had asked us to do. I'll never forget it. It was a deep experience of the word "joy" as it is used in the book of James. "Count it all joy, my brothers, when you meet trials of various kinds" (James 1:2).

Obediently Following Jesus

As Jesus commissioned His disciples, He instructed them to make more disciples who would obey everything He had commanded (Matthew 28:20). Jesus loves us. And it's out of love for Him that we obey. James tells us that "faith by itself, if it does not have works, is dead" (James 2:17). This is one of the main themes in the book of James: faith in action. But something to keep in mind is that obedience can involve and require risk. Those risks may not always be as tangible as in our story, but they are still felt. In radical abandonment of the desires of this world to follow Jesus, you may be faced with making decisions that family members, peers, or employers do not understand, even oppose. Or you may be faced with much greater sacrifice.

By faith we take radical steps of obedience. And by taking those steps of obedience, we are given the opportunity for our faith to be strengthened. Our faith is about more than just believing something—it requires a submission to God that includes submitting to whatever He has for our lives.

Read the following verses. Describe what it looks like to be an obedient follower of Jesus.

James 1:22

James 1:25

James 1:27

James 2:22

James 3:2

James 3:17

James 4:15, 17

James 5:16

We read in James 1:27 that we are to care for widows and orphans. And as we have already seen, loving our neighbor was certainly important to Jesus. But notice how in James 1:18 we are told that "of his own will he brought us forth by the word of truth, that we should be a kind of *firstfruits* of his creatures" (emphasis mine). This fruit has to do with salvation, and "firstfruits" implies that there will be a second, third, fourth, and so on—a continuing harvest to be brought in. Thus, we are called to be involved in spreading the gospel through both Great Commandment and Great Commission ministries.

Trials and Persecution

It's also important to take all of this in the context of how the book of James begins and ends—encouraging believers through trials and persecution. If knowing and doing the right thing were easy, we wouldn't need so much instruction from the Bible. There will be difficult decisions, hardships, and obstacles ahead. But James told us to "Count it all joy, my brothers, when you meet trials of various kinds" (James 1:2).

Read the verses below. Discuss what these passages teach about the trials ahead.[1]

James 1:2; 1 Peter 4:12

James 1:3

James 1:4

James 1:12

James 5:11; Job 1:6-12; Luke 22:31-32

Jesus warned His disciples of danger ahead. The night of Jesus' arrest, Peter went through a trial—a sifting like wheat—that Jesus permitted in order to strengthen his faith and that of other believers (Luke 22:31-34). Then, shortly after receiving the Holy Spirit, Peter and John were arrested for proclaiming and teaching about Jesus, which provided an opportunity for even deeper surrender. Once they were released, they reported to their friends the threats they had received. They all stopped, acknowledged God's greatness, accepted His plan, and pleaded for courage to continue sharing His story (Acts 4:24-29). Though they undoubtedly experienced growth through these trials, the purpose of a trial is not primarily that. Rather, just as we saw when Peter and John's friends responded by acknowledging God's greatness, trials are ultimately for God's glory to be seen.

"Submit yourselves therefore to God. Resist the devil, and he will flee from you. Draw near to God, and he will draw near to you" (James 4:7-8a). Living an obedient life is made possible by the transforming work of the Spirit in and through your life. "To those who are elect ... according to the foreknowledge of God the Father, in the sanctification of the Spirit, for obedience to Jesus Christ and for sprinkling with his blood: May grace and peace be multiplied to you" (1 Peter 1:1-2).

Healthy Living

Our spiritual health is intertwined with our emotional and physical well-being. Sometimes the signs of being unhealthy emotionally and physically reveal the health and inner-working of your spiritual being. But as you examine yourself and aim to maintain a healthy lifestyle, seek to do so not because you must or should but because you *want* to.[2]

My wife and I have lived in numerous countries, cultures, and homes. It's true that you can find things to complain about anywhere—and at times we have! We've lived in places with frequent power outages, inconsistent water supplies, extreme poverty, political tension, harsh winters, seemingly constant downpours, as well as smells, sights, and sounds that were unfamiliar and often unwelcome. We've also lived in a place where most of those things weren't issues. Being far from friends, family, and community is consistently our greatest difficulty with any move. There are always challenges in the midst of adjustment.

Expectations

We have found that our success in adjusting well to new places, people, and cultures often comes down to our attitude. If we humbly seek to understand the culture and embrace the differences that do not violate Scripture, then generally our adjustment is smooth and our relationships are fruitful. You can choose to be content, and you can choose to have gratitude. You are in control of your attitude, your actions, and your reactions. As we look back, we can see that as we chose to embrace the people and places God sent us to, He used the challenges in constructive ways to help us grow in our relationship with Him and with others.

Read 1 Peter 4:7-11. Discuss your expectations with the questions below.

How can you apply this passage to your personal expectations?

What do you expect from your teammates and ministry partners?

What do you expect from the local community where you are going to serve?

What do you expect will be different about where you are going to serve from where you live or where you've been before?

Examination
Read 1 Peter 2:11-12. Discuss our struggle with the flesh, using the questions below.

What do your identity and image have to do with self-control?

What are signs of being physically unhealthy? Emotionally unhealthy? Spiritually unhealthy?

How do you have an honorable witness?

How can you protect yourself from being hindered—spiritually, emotionally, and physically—and strive to be holy in all aspects of your life?

- -

The work is not a pretty thing, to be looked at and admired. It is a fight. And battlefields are not beautiful. But if one is truly called of God, all the difficulties and discouragements only intensify the call. If things were easier there would be less need. The greater the need, the clearer the call rings through one, the deeper the conviction grows: it was God's call. And as one obeys it, there is the joy of obedience, quite apart from the joy of success. There is joy in being with Jesus in a place where His friends are few.

—AMY CARMICHAEL, *THINGS AS THEY ARE* [3]

SURRENDER

Review
Use the following questions to briefly review the content of this week's study.

What did you learn about being an obedient follower of Jesus?

What did you learn about the risks, trials, and hardships that will come?

What expectations do you have?

How does your physical, emotional, and spiritual health put you in a better or worse position to obey?

Response + Prayer
In groups of two or three, discuss the following questions.

How are you actively seeking to live an obedient life?

What are your biggest struggles in the areas of physical, emotional, and spiritual health?

What did you take away from this week's study? What will you do in response?

What prayer requests do you have?

How can we pray for our community?

How can we pray for the people we are going to serve?

Spend some time praying together.

YOUR PLAN: OBEY

WHERE ARE YOU AT?

How have you been obeying what the Bible teaches and what the Spirit has placed on your heart?

WHERE ARE YOU GOING?

What do you need to be spending your time on? List all the ideas you have below.

From the list above, underline the things that need to be acted on within the next year. Circle the most important things to act on within the next three months.

TEAM MEAL ON A SHORT-TERM TRIP.

LOVE

This is my commandment, that you love one another as I have loved you. JOHN 15:12.

You shall love your neighbor as yourself. MATTHEW 22:39.

In this session, we will explore how to carry out Jesus' command to love one another. We must recognize that we each bring different experiences, personalities, convictions, and skill sets to the table. We should be speaking life into one another—out of love, encouraging each other to grow as He has wired, called, and gifted each of us. And we should strive to work in a spirit of unity so that as one we may glorify God. Here's the main idea:

> The love of Christ should compel us to make every effort to genuinely care for the people around us and around the world.

SESSION OUTLINE
- True Community
- Imitators of God
- Conflict
  - Reactions
  - Resolving Conflict
  - Reconciliation

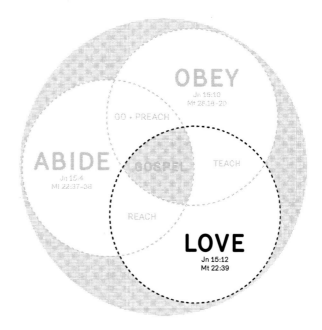

START

Welcome to this week's small-group meeting.

How are you?

How are you doing? How are we doing?

What has God been teaching you?

How have you obeyed what we discussed last week?

Did you share the gospel with anyone this week? How did it go?

Worship + Parable Study

Spend some time worshipping God together in song.

Read Luke 15:11-32, "The Prodigal Son."

What is the main message of this parable?

What does the parable tell us about how the kingdom grows?

What is our part?

What should we expect and how should you respond?

STUDY

LJ was able to make the hard road from a poor mountain village to a university in the city.[1] He is a godly young man of humility and maturity, so I was shocked when he told me his story. Due to the location of his remote village home, by age 11 he was living in a dormitory at a county-level boarding school. He was raising himself from a young age, which resulted in a life of heavy drinking, fighting, and causing trouble in the local community—and he had the scars to prove it.

The first time LJ heard about Jesus was during his freshman year in college. At that time, he blew it off, thinking "it sounded a bit ridiculous." Later that year, a teacher woke him up from his wild life—warning that if he didn't calm down, he'd likely find himself in an early grave. The next year, a friend brought him to an underground house church. When he saw that group of believers, he was amazed—their lives were totally different from his. He wanted to know more. One of the leaders began meeting with him on a daily basis, and three weeks later LJ began to follow Jesus. His life was never the same.

The night before Jesus' arrest, He gave his disciples a new commandment, "Love one another." He went on to say that "By this all people will know that you are my disciples, if you have love for one another" (John 13:35). The house church that LJ visited is one that we worked very closely with for a number of years. Of all the images we had for what biblical church should look like, they were it!

True Community

A true community that genuinely reflects Jesus is more than a group of believers just gathering together. It's about disciples of Jesus bonding together with a common identity and purpose—living out life and mission together. That's what we yearn for. And it's this same bond that we see in the early church as they united around an identity that they called the Way (Acts 9:2; 24:14). Likewise, we recognize that what will bring us together as such a community is a simple and determined dedication to follow Jesus—one way, one truth, one life (John 14:6).

Think back on your experiences in discipleship groups and churches. How would you define true community?

Read Romans 12:9-21; Ephesians 4:1-3. As a true community, what should we be and not be? What should we do and not do?

Read Ephesians 4:4-6. What is the common identity that we rally around in such a community?[2]

Imitators of God

We love because He first loved us (1 John 4:19). God's love helps us to understand love, and only His love can help us to more and more consistently love one another. He helps us to look beyond ourselves to follow His example and focus our attention on building each other up.

Read Ephesians 5:1-2. Who should we imitate? What did He do?

Read Ephesians 5:8-17. What are some ways that we can live as imitators of God?

Read Ephesians 5:17-21. How should our lives be filled?

Read Ephesians 5:21-6:9. Who are some of the people we should act lovingly toward?

Read Ephesians 6:10-20. How do we become this kind of person and be this type of community?

Conflict

When it comes to relationships, our focus must remain on God. We must continually allow Him to transform us to be loving people. However, just ending the conversation talking about the need to love one another may not be enough. Having experienced the reality of conflict, I recognize that being in the midst of division is not easy. Individual and cultural differences are a reality—there will be interpersonal challenges. Conflict can come at unexpected times and from unexpected sources. When situations arise, you need to know how to handle conflict and you need to be prepared to do it well.

Reactions

Read James 4:1. Discuss how you react to conflict, using the following questions.

How do you generally respond to conflict? Do you shut down and bottle everything up? Do you become aggressive and combative?

What problems have you had when you didn't seek to resolve conflict or you didn't react well?

How can you resist the temptation to either explode or shut down?

Resolving Conflict

Read Matthew 18:15-20; Ephesians 4:26-27. Discuss using the following questions.

If someone is in sin or has wronged you and it requires confrontation, what should you do?

If you confront someone and they don't accept what you say or change as a result, then what should you do?

Read Philippians 2:4; Colossians 3:12-17. Discuss using the following questions.

How should followers of Jesus act toward each other?

What are you responsible for?

Consider and discuss the following suggestions about how to confront well.

- **Be a peacemaker:** "And let the peace of Christ rule in your hearts, to which indeed you were called in one body" (Colossians 3:15a). Confrontation must be motivated and driven by love.

- **Be prayerful:** Before you confront, pray for the person(s) and the situation. Pray about your attitude, motives, timing, the words you will you use, and the way you will communicate.

- **Be aware:** Examine yourself first. What are you fearful of or worried about? What distortions might you have about the other person? Are you bitter? Are you tired? Remember Jesus' words about judging others. "Why do you see the speck that is in your brother's eye, but do not notice the log that is in your own eye? Or how can you say to your brother, 'Let me take the speck out of your eye,' when there is the log in your own eye? You hypocrite, first take the log out of your own eye, and then you will see clearly to take the speck out of your brother's eye" (Matthew 7:3-5).

- **Be assuring:** Affirm and validate the other person and have an attitude of humility. If applicable to the situation, apologize and ask for forgiveness for how you contributed to or caused the problem.

- **Be clear:** "Brothers, if anyone is caught in any transgression, you who are spiritual should restore him in a spirit of gentleness. Keep watch on yourself, lest you too be tempted" (Galatians 6:1). We have a responsibility to confront—but make sure that this is done with love, gentleness, and grace. Try to be specific about the problem, its effects, and your desire to help.

- **Be calm:** Think about how you will respond to counterattack, anger, or blame. "Know this, my beloved brothers: let every person be quick to hear, slow to speak, slow to anger; for the anger of man does not produce the righteousness of God" (James 1:19-20).

- **Be a listener:** When we are emotional, our ability to reason becomes limited. Try to remain calm and make sure that you hear the other person correctly. Many counselors recommend that after listening but before responding, you say back to the person what you just heard. For example, you might say, "What I hear you saying … ." Similarly, if someone reacts negatively to you, ask them to repeat what they heard you say. You might respond like this, "I'm sorry, I think I may have miscommunicated something. Can you tell me what you just heard me say?"

- **Be a learner:** Work on learning skills for dealing with conflict and seek wise counsel from mature believers—we always have room to improve in this area. There are also a number of quality books and resources available for growing in the area of interpersonal relationships.[3]

Reconciliation
Read 2 Corinthians 5:14-16 and discuss the following questions.

What does this tell us about who we are?

What does this tell us about how we should seek to view others?

- -

As we build up and enjoy one another, we are in fellowship, but as we join together to spread the gospel, we are in partnership and our objectives are focused outside ourselves on those who need to be brought into the fellowship of God's people.

—Jerry Bridges, *True Community*[4]

SURRENDER

Review
Use the following questions to briefly review the content of this week's study.
What does true community look like?
How do we live as imitators of God?
What did you learn about carrying out Jesus' commands to love one another?
What did you learn about handling conflict?

Response + Prayer
In groups of two or three, discuss the following questions.
How are your relationships?
Where do you struggle in expressing love and care toward others?
What did you take away from this week's study? What will you do in response?
What prayer requests do you have?
How can we pray for our community?
How can we pray for the people we are going to serve?

Spend some time praying together.

YOUR PLAN: LOVE

WHERE ARE YOU AT?

How is your relationship with your immediate family?

How is your relationship with the people you work with and/or go to school with?

How is your relationship with the rest of your family? Friends? Church? Others in your community?

WHERE ARE YOU GOING?

Where are you weak? What actions do you need to take to keep your relationships healthy? What do you need to do to restore relationships that are unhealthy?

MAKE DISCIPLES

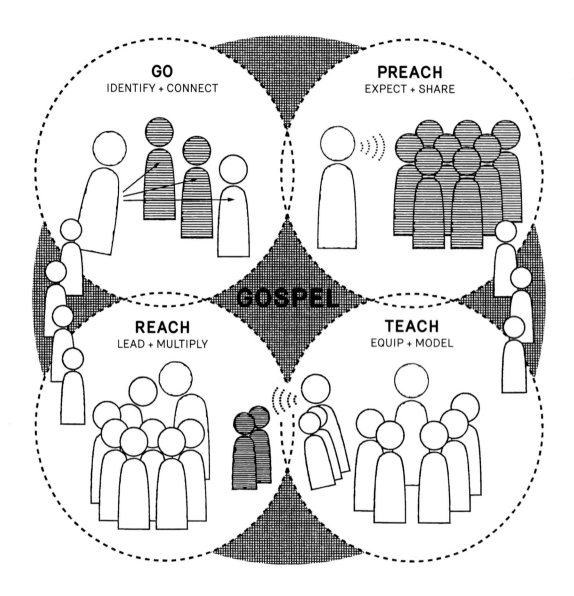

For as the earth brings forth its sprouts, and as a garden causes what is sown in it to sprout up, so the Lord God will cause righteousness and praise to sprout up before all the nations. ISAIAH 61:11

There is a well-known account given in Luke 10 where Jesus sent 72 of His followers ahead of Him into an area called Judea. In it, He provided direction for their mission, beginning with the famous verse, "The harvest is plentiful, but the laborers are few." He then urged them to pray, "Therefore pray earnestly to the Lord of the harvest to send out laborers into his harvest" (Luke 10:2). Jesus used the illustration of farming often, such as in the parable of the sower. In the sessions that follow, we will examine the mission process[1] as four steps in the harvest,[2] centered and founded on the gospel, as introduced below:

Go: Identify + Connect
Entering the harvest fields: In the parable of the sower, the first thing the farmer did was to go out (Mark 4:3).
- **go** *v.* take the gospel to the lost
- **identify** *v.* understand the people and their needs
- **connect** *v.* personally know and be engaged in people's lives

Preach: Expect + Share
Sowing the seeds of the gospel: In the parable of the sower, the farmer indiscriminately scattered the seed (Mark 4:4-8a).
- **preach**[3] *v.* provide an opportunity for the lost to hear the gospel
- **expect** *v.* have confidence that the Spirit will guide you and convict the lost
- **share** *v.* make the gospel message known and invite a response

Teach: Equip + Model
The seed comes up and grows: In the parable of the sower, the seed that fell on good soil "and produced a crop" (Mark 4:8a, HCSB).
- **teach** *v.* instruct believers in how to grow in godliness and make disciples
- **equip** *v.* instruct believers in knowing and obeying the Word
- **model** *v.* 1) be an example of Jesus, 2) show in action how to live and be on mission

Reach: Lead + Multiply
The harvest multiplies: In the parable of the sower, the seed grew and produced a crop "that increased 30, 60, and 100 times what was sown" (Mark 4:8b, HCSB).
- **reach** *v.* geographically saturate ethno-linguistic tribes with the gospel in an effort to make disciples who make disciples and churches that plant churches
- **lead** *v.* raise up leaders so that churches can stand on their own and continue the mission of making disciples
- **multiply** *v.* disciples of Jesus grow in godliness and reproduce themselves by making disciples of Jesus

SHEEP PEN AT A LOCAL PARTNER'S HOME.

GOSPEL-CENTERED MISSION

> But I do not account my life of any value nor as precious to myself, if only I may finish my course and the ministry that I received from the Lord Jesus, to testify to the gospel of the grace of God. ACTS 20:24

In this session,[1] we will explore our understanding of the gospel. We need to understand the context as we share the gospel, because individual and cultural factors are often different. We must understand the content, because the key elements of the gospel should always be communicated. And it is important to look at what the Bible says about the change that happens when someone becomes a follower of Jesus. Here is the main idea:

> The gospel must be our focus and foundation—we must be clear as we communicate the gospel and clear as we define it with those we work alongside.

SESSION OUTLINE
- The Context
  - Who is God?
  - Who are you?
  - What has God done?
  - What do you need to do?
- The Content
  - Jesus' Teaching on Eternal Life
  - The Big Picture
- The Change

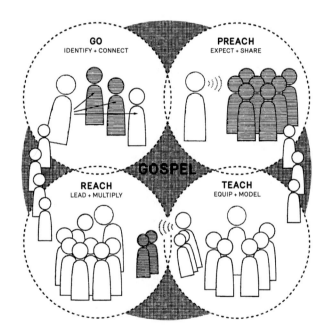

START

Welcome to this week's small-group study.

How are you?

How are you doing? How are we doing? What has God been teaching you?

How have you obeyed what we discussed last week?

Did you share the gospel with anyone this week? How did it go?

Worship + Parable Study

Spend some time worshipping God together in song.

Read Mark 4:3-20, "The Sower and the Soils."

What is the main message of these parables?

What do these parables tell us about how the kingdom grows?

What is our part?

What should we expect and how should you respond?

STUDY

We are all at different points in our journey, but before moving forward I want to make sure that we are on the same page about the one thing on which all of our hope rests: the gospel of Jesus Christ. If you are participating in a study like this, then I assume that you confess to know and believe the gospel.

So now, I want to ask a question: What is the gospel?

Many disciples of Jesus, and even many disciple leaders, have admitted difficulty in answering this question. We need to ask if we can provide an answer to this question for someone who isn't following Jesus. We need to know—we *must* know—the gospel. And we need to be ready to share it clearly.

In a few sentences or a paragraph, how would you share the gospel with someone who is not a follower of Jesus?

If you are a follower of Jesus, then you already have the word of faith (Romans 10:8). And since God gave us the responsibility to preach the gospel to those who have not heard (Romans 10:14-15), we should examine whether we can share our faith clearly. As gospel-centered disciples, we should understand three things: the context in which we share the gospel, the content of the gospel, and the change in one who becomes a follower of Jesus.

The Context

It is commonly known that gospel means good news. But what is good news to the people you are taking the gospel to? It is possible for all sorts of things to be good news that aren't the gospel. So how does the good news fit into their lives?

Beliefs about origins, reality, existence, morality, and eternity all impact a culture's worldview. These are good things to know. And knowing these things will help you grow as a communicator of the gospel—but worldview issues can get complex. I have often heard others who have been active in evangelism arrive in a new location and express a sense of being overwhelmed, not knowing how to even begin sharing the gospel. When the prevailing worldview is extremely different from yours, it can feel like it might take forever to be in a position to say anything. So I like to ask, "On a practical and individual level, how will you connect with people?" For some, talking about such worldview topics may hit the spot and lead to a meaningful presentation of the gospel. For most, the connection likely will be something else.

Often, communicating the gospel well comes down to connecting on a personal level—such a connection may get into worldview, but more importantly it will get to the heart. You're not aiming to speak just on a surface level but instead to really dig down into others' hearts and lives. It could be that they are searching for hope or consumed by fear. It could be that they are struggling with pride, selfishness, identity, loneliness, insecurity, abuse, addiction, hatred, prejudice, oppression, suffering, shame, sickness, desire, poverty, greed, immorality, dishonor, or disrespect. Or they could just simply be searching for something relevant. These aren't issues to ignore. Instead, these are issues to acknowledge. Use them to point people to true faith, true hope, and true love. Ask questions that provide the opportunity to open up about the struggles or desires in life, and make sure you hear what they are saying—get to know people. This is a great way to grow in your understanding of other people and how to communicate in their context.

Next, we need to think about where the gospel fits in. Regardless of the context, always try to answer four questions when presenting the gospel.[2]

> Who is God?
> Who are you?
> What has God done?
> What do you need to do?

The answers to these questions are found throughout the pages of Scripture. In our study, we're going to look at the church in Ephesus as an example. This should help us to examine not only how we can connect on a personal level but also, more importantly, how the gospel connects on a personal level. Acts 19-20 describes the scene: the people were of both Jewish and pagan Greek backgrounds—some having a worldview that included God, others having one that was far from God. If you remember the story, during Paul's ministry there, the Word mightily spread and saturated the entire province! For three years he did not cease passionately "testifying both to Jews and to Greeks of repentance toward God and of faith in our Lord Jesus Christ" (Acts 20:21; cf. 20:31). But this greatly threatened a number of people, which led to some serious opposition. Early on, it was at the Jewish synagogue. But later, Paul's time in Ephesus was ended after a riot led by local idol makers and followers of the goddess Artemis. He later wrote a letter from prison to the believers in the region, proclaiming God's eternal purpose and plan for everyone everywhere.[3]

Who Is God?

In order to understand the gospel, it is essential to lay a foundation of who God is. For the same reason that Isaiah responded with humility and obedience upon seeing the Holy God, we need to communicate the greatness of God as a fundamental part of the gospel.[4]

Read Ephesians 1:16-23; 3:9. Who is God?

Who Are You?

We were created with a drive to worship. And in this pursuit, individuals, cultures, and religions attempt to resolve their problems or gratify their desires through seemingly endless means. Many come up with very elaborate beliefs, rules, and systems. Others can simply be seen to have a drive within them that leads to a never-ending chase after some thing, some experience, or some ambition that's bigger and better. In the secular realm, means of worship meant for God are given over to idolizing self, experiences, products, and people. So this drive to worship takes hold of more than just the so-called "religious" cultures and individuals—it also affects secular tribes and everyone in between.

In most contexts overseas and increasingly in Western cultures, the idea of sin can be a difficult and complex thing to explain. In fact, there are some people who are convinced that they have never done anything wrong.

Read Ephesians 2:1-3; 4:17-19. What is the bad news?

As I was studying Ephesians to write these lessons, I had an interesting conversation with a local East Asian man. He was well-read and had a strong interest in discussing religion and philosophy. In our conversation, I drew the three overlapping circles from the "Be a Disciple" section: abide, obey, and love. But rather than write abide, obey, and love, I changed the words to faith, works, and kindness. I asked him if all religions didn't basically teach these things. He immediately responded, "Yes." I left blank the center where the circles overlapped and asked him if anyone could hold all three of these things together perfectly. As this man was very well versed in religion, I was a little surprised by his response. He just stood there puzzled. Then after a long pause he said, "I don't know." I then began to tell him about Jesus.

I started trying the same approach with people from a variety of backgrounds in East Asia and South Asia. I even had the opportunity not long after this conversation to study Buddhist philosophy at a prominent institution and further test this. I found that for most people I interact with, talking about practicing faith, doing good works, and showing kindness immediately registers with them. When I then ask who can do all of this perfectly, it always provides an opportunity for me to share about Jesus and the message of the gospel.

Whether by faith in self, faith in the teaching of a religious system, or faith in any other system, everyone is trusting someone or something to come through, provide, sustain, and—knowingly or not—to be true. Whether they're talking about accomplishing something in this world, meeting religious requirements, or maintaining balance and harmony, many people say that they want to do good (at least by their own definition and estimation). We all know the desire but also the struggle to consistently show kindness toward others. Social projects are not just characteristic of the church—they are characteristic of humanity. The idea that we should be kind to one another is wired into all of us, but it is often the hardest of all virtues to truly live out.

What Has God Done?

When we look in the Bible, we find Someone who did live a perfect life. As we are made aware of what the bad news is, we are always pointed to the good news—the gospel of Jesus. Remember that Ephesians was written to both Jewish and Greek pagan-background believers. I think about that a lot as I share the gospel with people following a mixture of eastern religions and philosophies. When I read this letter, I hear Paul pointing people to Jesus by addressing these same three concepts of faith, works, and kindness.

Read Ephesians 3:11-12. What is the good news about placing our faith in Jesus?

Read Ephesians 2:10. What is the good news about trusting Jesus to help us do good works?

Read Ephesians 2:4-7. What is the good news about God's love?

Read Ephesians 1:13-14; 2:8-21. What has God done?

What Do You Need To Do?

We all know that the world is not as it should be. We need to communicate a biblical under-standing of who God is and who we are. Humbly chosen as God's vehicles to communicate the gospel, we must let people know everything isn't OK—but it can be.

Read Ephesians 4:21-24; 5:18-21. How should we respond?

The response is significant. Paul reminded those who had heard the gospel, likely claimed to believe the gospel, but didn't show the fruit of being transformed by the gospel what response to the gospel *should* look like. Our response to the gospel should include turning from every-thing corrupt in our lifestyle, our desires, and our relationships and turning to truly focus our minds on the things of God and worshipping Him.[5]

The Content

After the Last Supper, Jesus prayed a prayer that began with these words, "Father, the hour has come; glorify your Son that the Son may glorify you, since you have given him authority over all flesh, to give eternal life to all whom you have given him. And this is eternal life, that they know you the only true God, and Jesus Christ whom you have sent" (John 17:1b-3). Earlier in the same conversation He said, "Let not your hearts be troubled. Believe in God; believe also in me" (John 14:1). It was for this reason that John wrote his Gospel, "But these [records] are written so that you may believe that Jesus is the Christ, the Son of God, and that by believing you may have life in his name" (John 20:31).

Jesus' Teaching on Eternal Life

Let's now focus on the unchanging content of the gospel. Early in John's Gospel, we find the most well-known summary of the gospel in the Bible. "For God so loved the world, that he gave his only Son, that whoever believes in him should not perish but have eternal life" (John 3:16). You might remember that this statement came from a famous conversation that Jesus had with a religious leader named Nicodemus. It was a statement not only about God's love for the world but, as the following verses tell us, also a statement about the condemnation that *already* exists for anyone who does not believe in the only Son of God. Jesus taught about eternal life and how to have a relationship with God. It is vital to understand the difference between this story and all other stories—every aspect of true life comes only because of what Jesus has done.

Read the following verses. What did Jesus teach about eternal life?

John 5:24-30

John 6:35-40

John 10:7-11

John 12:24-26

John 14:5-6

John 20:24-29

The Big Picture

God's message to us runs as a single thread, cover to cover, through the Bible. The Bible is a message—a story about God—from God. As you study the Bible, I'd encourage you to look for this thread and seek to understand the overarching story of the Bible for yourself. And don't assume that the people you meet know anything about this story, this message of the gospel. Ask yourself how you can clearly point a nonbeliever to Jesus. How will you communicate the gospel so that all the pieces fit together—and fit into the story of their life?

With the big picture in mind, we need to identify the pieces—the stories, ideas, and truths—that we should include. To help guide us in our study, we are going to look at a few key statements about the gospel. Let's use these as a place to begin exploring the key elements that need to be included in a complete witness of the gospel.

Read Acts 13:26-39; Romans 1:1-4, 16-24 (see also 3:10-26); 1 Corinthians 15:1-8, 20-28; Galatians 3:8. Use the outline below as a guide for making note of the key stories, ideas, and truths that need to be in a complete gospel witness.

Who is God?
- The Bible—where the Message comes from
- God's nature + Creation

Who are you?
- The Fall—our sin nature

What has God done?
- The Rescuer—Jesus
- The Restoration—Jesus' promised return, judgment, and eternity

What do you need to do?
- Follow Jesus.
- Join with other believers.

The Change

During His conversation with Nicodemus, Jesus said that in order to enter the kingdom of God, one must be born again and born of the Spirit. Peter wrote that believers in Jesus are "born again to a living hope through the resurrection of Jesus Christ from the dead, to an inheritance that is imperishable, undefiled, and unfading, kept in heaven for you, who by God's power are being guarded through faith for a salvation ready to be revealed in the last time" (1 Peter 1:3b-5). Paul wrote to the Corinthians that "if anyone is in Christ, he is a new creation" (2 Corinthians 5:17a). The book of Ephesians provides numerous illustrations to help us better understand the change that occurs when Jesus becomes someone's Lord and Savior.

Read Ephesians 4:20-24. How do we change when we know Jesus?

Read Ephesians 1:4-6; 2:19-22. What are the illustrations of having life in Jesus?

Read Ephesians 3:14-19; 4:32-5:2. What is it like to follow Jesus?

A Conclusion

We don't want to risk complicating things here. It's not a matter of how good you are or aren't at presenting the gospel. If you are a follower of Jesus, you have the Spirit of God living in you. We should choose to think less about ourselves and lovingly tell others what the Word of God already says. Our faith in Jesus should drive us to live differently and to live intentionally. Every second of every day, people around the world are slipping into eternity separated from God— many having never heard the gospel even once.

As we go to make disciples, it is important that we know what the gospel is and what a complete witness of the gospel should include. The gospel does not change, but each culture, individual, and situation does—keep that in mind. Let your confidence rest in the fact that Jesus promised that His Spirit would convict the world and guide you in all truth (John 16:8-11, 13).

As we work side by side to make disciples of all nations, it is also important that we discuss and define this together. Working through these things and having a basic definition will not only help you grow as a communicator of the gospel, but it also should create a more consistent standard by which to hold each other accountable. Examine what the Word says and ask the Spirit to give you clarity and confidence in knowing how to communicate the gospel. "Now to him who is able to do far more abundantly than all that we ask or think, according to the power at work within us, to him be glory in the church and in Christ Jesus throughout all generations, forever and ever. Amen" (Ephesians 3:20-21).

Let's finish by asking the question again:[6]

In a few sentences or a paragraph, how would you share the gospel with someone who is not a follower of Jesus?

- -

Hear, you who are far off, what I have done; and you who are near, acknowledge my might.

—ISAIAH 33:13

SURRENDER

Review

Use the following questions to briefly review the content of this week's study.

What is the gospel? What are the key elements of the gospel?

What is good news to the people around you? What about the people group you are going to serve?

How will you share the gospel with the people around you? What about the people group you are going to serve?

Response + Prayer

In groups of two or three, discuss the following questions.

Where do you need to focus to grow as a disciple maker? In what areas are you weak?

Who do you know that needs to hear the gospel?

Who will you share the gospel with this week?

What did you take away from this week's study? What will you do in response?

What prayer requests do you have?

How can we pray for our community?

How can we pray for the people we are going to serve?

Spend some time praying together.

YOUR PLAN: GOSPEL-CENTERED MISSION

WHERE ARE YOU AT?

What are the core issues, desires, or fears of your people group?

How is your people group attempting to overcome or satisfy these issues?

WHERE ARE YOU GOING?

Considering your responses above, what would be good news to your people group?

How will you share the gospel with them? What tools or methods will you use?

KIDS PLAYING NEAR A MARKET TOWN.

GO: IDENTIFY + CONNECT

All authority in heaven and on earth has been given to me. Go therefore and make disciples of all nations. MATTHEW 28:18-19A

In this session, we will learn about entering into the harvest fields for the sake of the gospel (Mark 4:3, 14). Our first step in making disciples is to examine what we need to identify and understand about the lives, needs, and worldview of the people we are going to serve. To be effective, we must be intentional in how we live our life and connect with others. Here's the main idea:

> Whether our mission is to our community, country, or the continents,[1] we are dedicated to identifying physical and spiritual needs in an effort to genuinely connect with people and take the gospel to where they are.

Session Outline
- The Mission of the 12 and 72
- Identify
  - Getting There and Meeting People
  - Understanding Their Needs
  - Understanding Worldview and the Advance of the Gospel
- Connect
  - How to Learn from Them
  - How to Express Love for Others

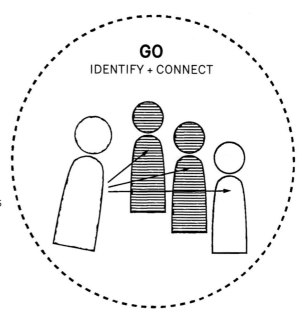

GO
IDENTIFY + CONNECT

START

Welcome to this week's small-group meeting.

How are you?

How are you doing? How are we doing?

What has God been teaching you?

How have you obeyed what we discussed last week?

Did you share the gospel with anyone this week? How did it go?

Worship + Parable Study

Spend some time worshipping God together in song.

Read Matthew 13:31-33, "The Mustard Seed and Leaven."

What is the main message of this parable?

What does the parable tell us about how the kingdom grows?

What is our part?

What should we expect and how should you respond?

STUDY

When my wife and I began our first overseas assignment, we had little more than scrap pieces of information left behind by the few who had come before us. We tried to ask everyone we met questions about our people group and areas. We searched on the Internet; we read books; we took notes. We started trying to go out and learn by riding buses to little market towns. But that didn't get us very far—most of our people group lived farther out. After about 10 months on the field, I was able to get a local driver's license. During a busy tourist season, we took the opportunity to rent a vehicle to explore isolated and remote areas. We drove up and down nearly every drivable road and path we could find asking questions, making notes, and marking places in our GPS. Over time, the Father provided more resources and partners—mostly nationals—who helped us to go deeper into the unreached pockets of our people group. But in the beginning, we had to fight hard just to know where to go and how to start.

Consider the scene at the giving of the Great Commission. "Now the 11 disciples went to Galilee, to the mountain to which Jesus had directed them. And when they saw him they worshipped him, but some doubted" (Matthew 28:16-17). We too need to be the ones who surrender with a heart of worship and follow Him and not be the ones who doubt. And we need to expect that His authority working through us will lead and carry us as we go to the people and places where He sends us—even when the task seems overwhelming.

The Mission of the 12 and 72[2]

Jesus sent His disciples out to prepare the way during His ministry. By studying these events, we can begin to learn about our mission, how we should prepare, and what we should expect.

Read Matthew 9:37-10:23; Luke 10:1-24. Discuss using the following questions.

What was their mission?

How were they equipped or prepared?

What were they to expect?

Identify

It is important for a disciple maker to be a lifelong learner. As you meet new people and enter new communities, prayerfully seek to understand their lives, their needs, and how to share the gospel with them. The rest of this section provides a number of questions to help you get started. Now isn't necessarily the time to answer all of these questions—you can refer to this later as you do further research. This is the time for us to get oriented with the topics and issues that we need to be on the lookout for.

Getting There and Meeting People

What do you need to understand about how to get to your people group and start building relationships? Discuss and consider the suggestions below.

- **Location:** Where do they live? Where are their population concentrations or segments?
- **Logistics:** How do you get to and from where they live? How do you get from one population segment to the next? How do you get around in your city or town? What are the available forms of local transportation?
- **Language:** What language do you need to communicate effectively? What language do they speak at home? What language(s) do they use in their community, market, and work (trade language(s))? How can you best communicate with them? Are they literate or nonliterate? If they are literate, do they learn primarily by literate or oral means?
- **Entry Points:** Where can you meet people? Where are they available? What are they interested in?
- **Availability:** When can you meet people? When are the times and seasons that people are available?
- **Access:** What are options for a sustained presence—often called a platform—among your people group?
- **Culture:** What is important to your people group? Do they identify more with traditions or trends? Are they focused on protecting the past or innovating for the future? Do they operate as individuals or groups? Is their concept of time punctual or fluid? How do they make decisions? How do they show honor and respect? How are their families typically structured? Is adultery, abuse, or addiction(s) common? How do people of different genders and classes interact? What are the customs when you are the guest? How do you politely accept something? How do you politely refuse something? What are the customs when you are the host? What are the significant events in their history? Who do they identify as being one of them?
- **Security:** Be prepared to answer these questions on a regular basis: Who are you? Why are you here? What do you do? Where do you get your money? How do you know him/her or each other?

Understanding Their Needs

Discuss how you might be able to meet physical needs in one or more of the following categories: poverty, hunger, food safety, addiction, abuse, widows, orphans, education, employment, and environmental hazards.

For most community development and disaster relief projects, it is important and wise to seek expert advice. The implementation of your project may require advanced training, certification(s), and/or government approval(s). Before jumping into a big project, consider how you might help in simple and economical ways first—often, the simple projects are the most successful. Develop a plan that can be carried out and sustained with local leaders and resources. Remember that foundational to your motivation to help the needy is the biblical mandate to make disciples. In your planning, make sure to determine how your project will facilitate the spread of the gospel and discipleship.

Understanding Worldview and the Advance of the Gospel

What do you need to understand to share the gospel with your people group? Discuss and consider the suggestions below.

- **Worldview:** What is most important to them? Who or what are they living for? What do they depend on? What are they afraid of? What do they do during major life events (such as birth, graduation, marriage, and death)? What do they believe happens after death? What are their places of worship (such as altars, monasteries, mosques, and temples)? What is the meaning of the religious objects they carry or have in their home? What are their beliefs? How do they talk about these things? Who in the culture is more concerned with religious things (such as the elderly, the men, the women, or the educated)? What is the significance of and meaning behind their festivals and holidays? What is their perception of Christianity—or do they even have one? Do they pray? If so, to whom and how?

- **Advance of the Gospel:** When you meet new people, are they lost or saved? (If they are lost, share the gospel with them; if they are saved, prayerfully determine if you can partner with them, encourage them, and/or teach them). What is the number or percentage of lost people among different segments of the people group or city? What areas have had less opportunity to hear the gospel? What areas have existing believers? Are there areas where people are receptive? Are there areas where there are visible signs of the Spirit at work? If there are churches, where are they, what are their beliefs, and what are they doing? Are there cults, or is there a history of cult activity? If so, what do the cults believe and teach; how do they do things? Have people heard of Jesus? Have people heard the gospel? Have people read the Bible? Who else is on mission for them?

Connect

Be personal and share your life with those you are sent to. "We cared so much for you that we were pleased to share with you not only the gospel of God but also our own lives, because you had become dear to us" (1 Thessalonians 2:8, HCSB). Whether we meet a lost person, a saved person, or are partnering with a church or other ministry, we need more than just book knowledge about their life and customs. What we really need is to spend time with them. We need to grow not only in how much we know about their culture but more importantly in how well we interact with the people of that culture. We need to love them and get to know what life is like for them—and we need to learn this from them.

How do we connect with people?

How to Learn from Them

Effectively connecting with people is a two-way street. It is often as much about patiently listening to them and learning from them as it is about actively speaking and engaging. "Let every person be quick to hear, slow to speak" (James 1:19b).

What should we be learning from the people we are sent to? Discuss and consider the following suggestions.

- **Interests:** Learn about what they do, what they enjoy, and where they go.
- **Stories:** Listen to their life stories about their community (such as village, country, culture, history, and religion), work (such as farming, factory, office, and studies), and family (such as personal life, parents, and children).
- **Hurts:** Be considerate of their struggles and hurts—everyone has them. We need to be sensitive as we communicate and interact. Be ready to listen and respond in a loving and biblical way if they share those parts of their lives.

How to Express Love for Others

We have to be willing to give up everything to genuinely express love toward others. It's like what Paul says in 1 Corinthians, "I have become *all* things to *all* people, that by *all* means I might save some. I do it *all* for the sake of the gospel" (1 Corinthians 9:22b-23a, emphasis mine). This is why we get out of our comfort zone to identify where people are and find entry points into their lives. It is the gospel that compels us to go to foreign and unfamiliar places where we don't understand the language, where we might think the food is strange, and where we might become frustrated with the culture and a different way of doing things. It is for the sake of the gospel.

What are some intentional things that you can do to express an interest in and care for others? Discuss and consider the following suggestions.

- **Be willing:** Be willing to embrace new things (such as eating their food, accepting their accommodations, using local forms of transportation, adopting appropriate styles of clothing, and learning their language).
- **Be noticeable:** You won't meet people staying in your home. Get out to where they are and plug into their community.
- **Be a servant:** We should help others. Find practical and economical ways to serve them (such as cleaning and other household work, inviting them to a meal, cooking for them, or buying them simple and practical gifts).
- **Be engaged:** Invite them in—not only to be a part of your ministry, but also to feel a part of your life.
- **Be available:** Make yourself accessible. Don't get too caught up in your to-do lists.
- **Be spontaneous:** Accept their invitations. Allow your routine to be unexpectedly interrupted.
- **Be flexible:** Follow their schedule. Be willing to proactively adjust or change your schedule to accommodate them (such as eating meals, going to bed, or having church at a different time).
- **Be fun:** Think creatively and host them, their family, and friends in your home or on an outing.
- **Be adaptable:** Learn how to do the games and activities that they do. Learn how to talk about the things that they talk about.
- **Be relational:** Be conversational and get to know their friends, family, and community.

The Spirit empowers us as we share the gospel and encourage believers. We must remember, His missional role is to convict; our missional role is simply to go. Love is the place where our going and His convicting converge. Since the Holy Spirit could do His work without us, why would He choose to use such imperfect instruments? Because His desire for an intimate relationship for us is so deep that He wants us to participate in His redeeming work. By the Spirit's presence, we can then be compelled by love to move out of our comfort zone and into the world where a hearing and demonstration of the gospel is needed.

—ED STETZER AND PHILIP NATION, *COMPELLED*[3]

SURRENDER

Review
Use the following questions to briefly review the content of this week's study.
What was the mission of the 12 and 72?

What did you learn to identify about the people you are going to serve?

What do you need to learn to identify about the worldview of your people group?

What did you learn about genuinely connecting with people on a personal level?

Response + Prayer
In groups of two or three, discuss the following questions.
What are some barriers—things you do or don't do that hinder your ability to connect—that you know you already have in your life?

What do you need to be intentional about doing or changing to better reflect Jesus?

What did you take away from this week's study? What will you do in response?

What prayer requests do you have?

How can we pray for our community?

How can we pray for the people we are going to serve?

Spend some time praying together.

YOUR PLAN: GO

WHERE ARE YOU AT?

List the segments that exist within your people group below, including geographic, economic, generational, vocational, and tribal interest groups.

From the list above, who are the most open? Who are the most closed? Who are being engaged with the gospel by others? Circle the top-priority segments to focus on this year.

WHERE ARE YOU GOING?

How often will you spend time with your people group this year? How many days per week, per month, and per year will you spend among the lost in your surrounding community? How many days per week, per month, and per year will you spend among the lost in more distant communities? Write a goal for where you will go and how often you will spend time with your people group.

What do you need to learn about your people group? Refer back to the session for examples, and list below the top things you need to identify. Write a goal for what you need to learn and research about your people group this year.

Review the section on connecting. What do you need to be mindful of as you interact with your people group? Write a goal for how you will strive to improve your interaction with people of different cultures and interests this year.

VILLAGE KID RIDING MY BIKE.

PREACH: EXPECT + SHARE

How then will they call on him in whom they have not believed? And how are they to believe in him of whom they have never heard? And how are they to hear without someone preaching? And how are they to preach unless they are sent? ROMANS 10:14-15A

In this session, we will learn about sowing the seed of the gospel (Mark 4:4-8, 14-20). The Spirit is at work convicting the lost and preparing hearts. We need to seek to see Him at work and to be ready to join in. As we find opportunities to share the gospel, we should know how to use our story, share His story, and invite a response. Here's the main idea:

Our aim is to actively articulate the gospel to the lost, expecting the Spirit to guide us and transform lives.

Session Outline
- Expect
  - Person of Peace
  - Being Expectantly Prepared
- Share
  - Share Your Story
  - Share His Story
  - The Process of Going and Sharing
  - Drawing the Net

PREACH
EXPECT + SHARE

START

Welcome to this week's small-group study.

How are you?

How are you doing? How are we doing?

What has God been teaching you?

How have you obeyed what we discussed last week?

Did you share the gospel with anyone this week? How did it go?

Worship + Parable Study

Spend some time worshipping God together in song.

Read Luke 14:12-24, "The Great Banquet."

What is the main message of this parable?

What does the parable tell us about how the kingdom grows?

What is our part?

What should we expect and how should you respond?

STUDY

Knowing what we know about God and the gospel should give us great confidence. "For God gave us a spirit not of fear but of power and love and self-control. Therefore do not be ashamed of the testimony about our Lord" (2 Timothy 1:7-8a, ESV). As we depend on His Spirit to help us boldly step out, we should strive to share His story as clearly as possible.

We should also keep in mind Paul's example. He told the Corinthian believers, "And I, when I came to you, brothers, did not come proclaiming to you the testimony of God with lofty speech or wisdom. For I decided to know nothing among you except Jesus Christ and him crucified ... and my speech and my message were not in plausible words of wisdom, but in demonstration of the Spirit and of power, so that your faith might not rest in the wisdom of men but in the power of God" (1 Corinthians 2:1-2, 4-5).

Expect

While training cross-cultural workers, a presenter showed the most recent *Global Status of Evangelical Christianity*[1] map and, somewhat in jest, said, "Look. Even in [*our unreached*] there are green dots!" Those green dots represented a level of 2 to 5 percent Christianity—which we knew to be completely wrong and grossly exaggerated for our location. We had been working there for a few years and my national partners were connected with every house church network in the area. Classic statistical error. We were the experts (so I thought). But I quickly came under deep conviction over my attitude. It was as though the Spirit gave me the thought that those dots may not represent what they claim they do, but they do represent something. This led to a shift in our strategy to aggressively spread the gospel—not only for the sake of the lost but also for the sake of finding isolated believers.

In one of my first trips out after this training, I felt burdened to go into a remote mountain location that seemed impossible to reach. Many people were out that day and although I was likely the first foreigner to come to some of those villages, few seemed interested in me—much less in hearing why I came. Discouraged, I finally started biking back through the villages. As I passed through a small stretch of houses, an old man yelled and waved me down. I knew that I needed to stop and spend some time with him. Soon into our conversation, he handed his granddaughter off and he pulled his stool closer to mine. He leaned over and in a quiet voice told me that He was a follower of Jesus. When I asked more, He gave me a beautiful presentation of the gospel. Fifteen years before, one of his family members went to work in a distant city and after returning told him about Jesus. In all, there were eight believers. They were afraid of persecution and knew of no other believers in the area. Over time, we were able to send others from their own people group to follow up with them.

This pattern continued over the following months as I began to frequently meet people in remote, unreached locations who had heard the gospel, had already believed, or knew of a nearby neighbor who did. I began to expect the Spirit to guide me and to see Him work—rather than primarily expecting difficulty and rejection. This sense of expectation changed my perspective whenever I went out into seemingly hopeless and remote areas.

Person of Peace

In our first session, we read in Isaiah that "the whole earth is full of [God's] glory" (Isaiah 6:3). Regardless of how big the barriers may seem, we can expect that His presence goes before us and that He will lead us to the people and places He would have us go. In many communities and people groups, it may feel like no one is receptive. It may feel hopeless and impossible. But we can have assurance that with God all things are possible (Matthew 19:26). We can rest in knowing that He is the one who does the work of salvation. Learn to follow Him where He is leading and join Him where He is at work. One of the ways He leads is by guiding us to prepared hearts.

Read the person of peace stories below and answer the following questions.

Luke 7:1-10 (The Centurion)

John 4:1-30 (The Samaritan Woman)

Acts 8:26-40 (The Ethiopian Eunuch)

Acts 10:9-11:1 (Cornelius)

Acts 16:13-15 (Lydia)

Acts 16:22-38 (The Philippian Jailer)

What patterns do you see in these person of peace examples?

How will we know who these prepared and open people are?

What is the difference between someone who welcomes our message versus someone who just welcomes us?

What are some ideas you have for finding persons of peace?

Whenever you see someone asking spiritual questions, open, or broken, that might be an indication of the Spirit's work in their life. Ask Him to give you spiritual eyes to see the way that He sees—learn to identify the harvest.[2] Be creative and stretch yourself in seeking new ways to find open and receptive people. Consider how you can follow the relationship lines of people you know—they might not be interested in the gospel, but they might have a friend or relative who is. How can you invite them into your life? How can you position yourself to be invited into theirs? Below are some suggestions for finding persons of peace.

Consider the following ideas for finding persons of peace and discuss:

- **Personal prayer:** Pray and ask for persons of peace to be brought to you.
- **Prayerwalking:** Pray in your people group's communities.
- **Prayer partners:** Send prayer requests to prayer partners and pray with colaborers.
- **People:** Get out and be with people. Spend time in strategic places and areas the Spirit has laid on your heart.
- **Purposely sow broadly:** Actively go to a broad number of places and people—as the adage goes, don't put all your eggs in one basket.
- **Proclaim the gospel:** Share the gospel—use the gospel as your filter.
- **Plan questions:** Ask questions about their passions, difficulties, and the things that are important to them. Ask if they are interested in learning about Jesus. Ask them if they know others who may be interested.
- **Response:** Invite them to respond to the gospel and invite them to study the Bible.
- **Reconnecting:** Ask for their contact information so that you can reconnect and continue the conversation.
- **Remember the Spirit:** Regardless of how you think it went, expect that the Spirit is at work bringing conviction and opening hearts—expect the unexpected.

We can be confident that Jesus goes with us, but we should be careful about our expectations. Remember how the farmer in the parable scattered the seed—he scattered it indiscriminately. It fell on the path, rocky ground, among thorns, and on good soil (Mark 4:4-8). I think that is the main lesson the Spirit taught me with those green dots. I was getting hung up by rejection and was not being as faithful as I should have been in sharing the gospel. The 12 and 72 were told to expect rejection and so are we. And though there is a pattern in the person of peace examples, we are not promised a Cornelius, Ethiopian eunuch, or Lydia out there waiting for us. When people don't give us an opportunity to share the gospel or don't seem interested, we need to know what to do. On the one hand, we must keep pushing ahead to find new people to share the gospel with (Matthew 10:23). On the other hand, we must seek the Spirit's guidance to keep sharing with some because salvation "depends not on human will or exertion, but on God, who has mercy" (Romans 9:16). What this comes down to is our responsibility to faithfully, obediently, and lovingly share the gospel.

Being Expectantly Prepared

As we go out on mission, it is important to recognize what is God's responsibility and what is our responsibility. It is He who guides and convicts. Only God can save. But He has given us certain responsibilities. We are encouraged to be ready to act as the Spirit leads, "always being prepared to make a defense to anyone who asks you for a reason for the hope that is in you" (1 Peter 3:15a).

How can you prepare to share the gospel? Discuss and consider the following.

- **Spiritual preparation:** The Spirit is always moving and working. Though there are some outward signs of openness, we must be sensitive to the Spirit's leading. Seek to daily abide in Jesus and His Word, pray throughout the day, and discern the guidance of the Spirit.
- **Study and practice sharing your story and His story:** Be prepared to share your story and His story. Daily read and study the Word. Be mentally ready to speak and spiritually sensitive to know when to act. When you can, carry Bibles and other literature or media with you to give to those you share with.

What should you do if someone believes? What should you do if you find a believer? Discuss and consider the following.

- **Equip new believers:** If someone you share with believes or if you find someone who is a believer, be prepared to immediately begin teaching them. Learn from other field workers how they are teaching new believers in your context or other similar contexts. Keep it simple and focused on obedience. (We will discuss more about teaching in "Teach: Equip + Model.")
- **Empower them to engage others:** Encourage them to share the gospel and their testimony with their friends and family and make disciples.

How can you make a plan to continue sharing the gospel? Discuss and consider the following.

- **Investment:** Stay active in sharing the gospel with new people but also depend on the Spirit to show you who is seeking so that you can invest more time in them.
- **Information:** Establish a method that works for you to write down and keep track of information. This may include names, dates, what was shared/taught, contact information, location information, and any additional notes that might be helpful. Have a plan for follow-up and try to execute it. Keep track of what you shared already and prayerfully think through what you will ask when you see them next.
- **Intercession:** "Devote yourselves to prayer, keeping alert in it with an attitude of thanksgiving" (Colossians 4:2, NASB). Pray as you prepare, pray for those you share the gospel with, and pray for those you teach.

- **Intentionality:** "making the most of the opportunity" (Colossians 4:5b). Be intentional in what you talk about when you follow up and plan to continue sharing His stories and your stories. Invite them to meet you at a regular time to study the Bible, and ask them if they have friends who may be interested.

Share

I doubt that you need the stats—take the population numbers for almost any unreached people group or city in the world and calculate in days and months and years what it is going to take to individually share the gospel with all of them. The reality of the number of people who have yet to hear the gospel is overwhelming. Our hearts should ache over this. At the same time, the love of God should compel us to do something about it. We must be clear: He has equipped and purposed all believers to be a part of this mission.

My wife and I have a burden to be urgent about sharing the gospel while also establishing long-term strategies. But I'll be honest—it's not always easy. Since moving overseas, my family and I have lived in three different countries, each work having its own unique challenges. With opportunity there is also struggle. At times, I want to make excuses for not sharing when I'm tired, busy, or think the timing is inconvenient. But we must be on watch to resist such temptations. We need to encourage one another to keep stepping out to passionately take the gospel to the lost, making the most of every opportunity—regardless of the cost. We should be prepared at all times to share His story—the gospel message. At the same time, we should also be ready to share our story.

Share Your Story

Your journey of how Jesus rescued you and changed your life has the potential to open doors for the gospel. It's hard to argue with a story, especially your own personal stories. So how do we tell our story?

Let's first look at the example of Paul.

Read Acts 26:1-29. How did Paul share his story? What did he include?

When we share our story, remember these three parts:

> What was your life like before Jesus?
> How did you meet Jesus?
> How has your life changed because of Jesus?

As you tell your story, remember why you are sharing it: the gospel. It was Paul's desire when sharing his testimony in Jerusalem that King Agrippa and all who heard him that day would become followers of Jesus, just as he was (Acts 26:28-29). Consider how you can be intentional to use your story to communicate His story—the gospel.

When sharing your story, you may focus on different aspects—each aspect true but each adapted to address the themes and experiences most appropriate for different individuals. Understanding a little bit about the person you are talking with will probably help your story connect in a more meaningful way (as discussed in Session 6 "Go: Identify + Connect").

Using the following questions, discuss other details and experiences that you may want to consider as you share your story.

What other stories from your life may connect with others? What difficult experiences have you gone through? How has Jesus made a difference?

What are some common themes that may resonate with your people group (such as success, poverty, pressure, complacency, pride, fear, loss, sickness, broken relationships, worry, addiction, abuse, injustice)?

Different situations and different people will allow different lengths of time to share your story. What will you share if you only have two minutes? What will you focus on if you have 10 minutes or longer? How will you use your story to bridge to His story?

Share His Story

If you are a follower of Jesus, you have the Spirit of God living in you—and you have the best story to tell. It should be a natural overflow of our lives to share the gospel. As we go to make disciples, we need to examine whether we are clear about what the gospel is and what a complete witness of the gospel should include. There are many tools available for sharing the gospel. If they help, use them—they can be very helpful ways to grow as a disciple maker. Whatever methods for sharing the gospel you consider, always take everything back to the Word—let it be your authority and let the Spirit be your guide.

In any situation, it is important to lovingly and genuinely connect on a personal level with others. Be willing to have open and vulnerable, two-way conversations and allow your life to be seen in light of the gospel. Below we're going to highlight some verses to further guide and encourage us as we share His story.

Read John 15:7-8; 2 Peter 3:17-18. How can you stay committed to biblical integrity as you make disciples?

Read 1 Peter 3:15. How should you engage the lost with the gospel?

Read Acts 14:11-18; 21:40-22:2; Revelation 5:9. How can you communicate effectively?

Read Romans 10:14; Ephesians 1:13. Whether your people group is literate, semi-literate, oral, or deaf, how should you communicate the gospel?

Read Luke 24:13-27, 44-49; Acts 17:22-34. Where should you start in the biblical narrative? What stories, ideas, and truths should you include?

Read 2 Corinthians 3:4-6. Why can we have confidence when we share the gospel?

Read 2 Corinthians 4:1-5 (see also 3:12-18). How are we to boldly share the gospel?

Get with others who are burdened for the same or similar people groups. Learn from each other and encourage each other to stay focused and active.

Consider the following questions to ask partners and mentors.

- **Bridges:** What topics work well for starting a conversation? How do you change, or bridge, the conversation to the gospel?
- **Barriers:** What struggles or challenges have you faced sharing the gospel? Are there certain topics, stories, or other issues that seem to create a significant barrier when sharing the gospel?
- **Best tools:** What methods do you recommend for sharing the gospel? How have you adapted common evangelism tools for your context? Do you have training or materials available?
- **Calling for response:** How do you invite nonbelievers to respond to the gospel?
- **Continued investment and follow-up:** How do you continue to invest in nonbelievers who are open to the gospel? What information about them and your time together do you record? How do you handle follow-up?

The Process of Going and Sharing

We know that "the word of God is living and active, sharper than any two-edged sword, piercing to the division of soul and of spirit, of joints and of marrow, and discerning the thoughts and intentions of the heart" (Hebrews 4:12). But sometimes one of our main challenges is just starting a conversation and getting to the point of being able to share the gospel.

Considering your context, where are places to find or meet people (the entry places)?

What are some questions you can use to start a conversation? Discuss and consider the following suggestions.[3]

- **Food:** What do you like to eat? Where are your favorite places to eat? What would you recommend? Would you teach me to cook [a local food]? Can I teach you to make [your food]?
- **Family:** Where are you from? What about your family? What's your mom like? What does your dad do? Do you have any siblings? Do you get to see them or talk with them much?

- **Festivals:** What are your major holidays and festivals? What do your festivals celebrate? Who do you get together with in your community? Do you do anything charitable?
- **Friends and Fun:** What are you interested in? What kinds of groups are you involved in? What is your favorite music? What sports or activities do you enjoy? What do you read?
- **Free Time:** When do you have time? When do you get off work? Do you want to join us? Do you want to get together for a meal, tea, or coffee?
- **Full Time:** What do you do? What is your major?
- **Faith:** Are you a Hindu, Buddhist, Muslim, or atheist? Tell me what you believe—I want to understand why you believe what you believe. Do you know any Christians? Have you ever heard of Jesus? Can I tell you a story?
- **Familiar:** What is that? How do you say that in [*local language*]? How do you do that? What are they doing? Why?
- **Friendly:** Can I help you with that?

What are some ideas you have for transitioning—or bridging—the conversation to the gospel? Discuss and consider the suggestions below.

- **Ask lots of questions:** Be interested and engaged in what they want to talk about and get to the heart of why that is or is not important to them. The more you dialogue, the more you will recognize, with the help of the Spirit, natural bridges to change the conversation to the gospel.
- **Bring up everyday topics:** Be thinking through everyday topics (such as relationships, family, beliefs, life successes, and current events) and how you can move the conversation to sharing your story and His story.
- **Connect with Bible Stories:** Be listening for anything in the conversation that may remind you of a Bible story, a parable, a passage, or a testimony of how God worked in your life.

Drawing the Net

Jesus called His first disciples saying, "Follow me, and I will make you fishers of men" (Matthew 4:19).[4] As disciples of Jesus, we too are called to be fishers of men. It is one thing to cast out the net by sharing the gospel, but like any fisherman you also need to draw the net back in.

Jesus began His ministry "proclaiming the gospel of God, and saying, 'The time is fulfilled, and the kingdom of God is at hand; repent and believe in the gospel'" (Mark 1:14-15). He ended His ministry, in Luke's account, instructing His disciples and commanding that "repentance and forgiveness of sins should be proclaimed in his name to all nations" (Luke 24:47). And, in Matthew's account, He commanded to "make disciples of all nations, baptizing them in the name of the Father and of the Son and of the Holy Spirit" (Matthew 28:19). Though it was not recorded in every instance in the book of Acts, we can safely assume that when the gospel was shared, there was an expectation and call to respond. Paul lived his life "testifying both to Jews and to Greeks of repentance toward God and of faith in our Lord Jesus Christ" (Acts 20:21). We are to call people to turn from the gods of this world and turn to the God of the universe. We have a responsibility to clearly communicate that response to the gospel requires repentance and faith.

How can you intentionally and clearly invite someone to follow Jesus?

We must be clear as we call people to follow Jesus. And we must not make assumptions with this. I moved overseas with many opinions about what a call to respond needed to be. Over time, I became confused and frustrated with people seemingly understanding the story of the gospel but not its ramifications for them personally. My heart was greatly burdened for these unreached people and I pleaded daily with God for their salvation. In my brokenness, I became desperate and grew open to try any approach that might help them see the relevance of this gospel that was so foreign to them. For a few months, I prayerfully tried a range of methods from those I was cynical about to those I was convinced were perfectly tailored for rural, oral people groups. I tried multiple approaches with the same people in the same conversation. I tried placing invitations at the beginning, middle, and end of sharing the gospel. What did I find? I saw people understand the gospel using all of these methods, at least sometimes. What the Spirit taught me through this was significant. Most importantly, He humbled me about my preconceived ideas and theories. He showed me that it was much less about method and much more about depending on Him. I had to be constantly willing and ready to clearly communicate the gospel and make a call to respond.

In different cultures, languages, generations, and minds, concepts like repentance, belief, trust, and faith are understood differently. What communicates clearly with one person might not with the next. It's not about specific words or techniques as much as it's about actively working to make known that the one true God demands all people everywhere to turn from everything and follow Him. Just as one thing is necessary for us, one thing is necessary for the people we are sent to. Your responsibility is to clearly and faithfully share the gospel and call people to repent and follow Jesus—God is the One who brings conviction and salvation. In order to be ready to share the gospel, it is critical that you prayerfully spend time in the Word, internalize its message, and keep it fresh on your mind and heart.

In a very real and sobering way, we must actually become the gospel to the people around us—an expression of the real Jesus through the quality of our lives. We must live our truths. Or as Paul says it, we ourselves are living letters whose message is constantly being read by others (2 Corinthians 3:1-3).

—ALAN HIRSH, *THE FORGOTTEN WAYS*[5]

SURRENDER

Review
Use the following questions to briefly review the content of this week's study.

What did you learn about persons of peace? How can you prepare to share the gospel?

How can you make a plan to follow up with the people you share the gospel with?

What did you learn about sharing your story?

What did you learn about sharing His story?

What did you learn about drawing the net?

Response + Prayer
In groups of two or three, discuss the following questions.

What evangelism tools have you used before?

What evangelism approaches would you consider to be appropriate for the people in your community? What about for the people group you are going to serve?

Consider the graph below. What step(s) in the process of going and sharing will be the biggest challenge for you?

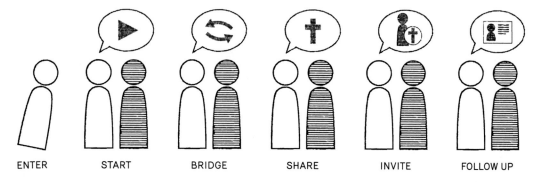

| ENTER | START | BRIDGE | SHARE | INVITE | FOLLOW UP |

What do you need to do to help you grow as a fisher of men?

What did you take away from this week's study? What will you do in response?

What prayer requests do you have?

How can we pray for our community?

How can we pray for the people we are going to serve?

Spend some time praying together.

PLAN: PREACH

WHERE ARE YOU AT?

List the tools or methods commonly being used to proclaim the gospel with people groups similar to the one(s) you are serving. Next, underline the tools you consider clear and reproducible. Then, circle the one underlined tool in which you will seek to become proficient this year.

List the materials and media available for distribution in your people group's language(s) (such as Bibles, gospel tracts, booklets, The *JESUS* Film, The Hope, The Prophets' Story, and God's Stories). Then, circle the resources that will be most helpful to use when sharing the gospel.

WHERE ARE YOU GOING?

How will you pray for the salvation of your people group? How will you send requests to prayer partners? How will you pray with locals? Write a goal for how you will pray for your people group this year.

Write a goal for how you will study and practice sharing your story and His story.

How will you track the contact information of those you share with for follow-up? What information will you record?

Write a goal for how many times per week, per month, and per year you will share the gospel.

If no tools or resources are available in the heart language of your people group, then list one or two tools you could work to have translated this year.

TRAINING LOCALS BEFORE SENDING THEM OUT.

TEACH: EQUIP + MODEL

Teaching them to observe all that I have commanded you. And behold, I am with you always, to the end of the age. MATTHEW 28:20, ESV

In this session, we will learn about our role when the seed comes up, grows, and produces a crop (Mark 4:8, 20). Jesus instructed us in the Great Commission to teach disciples to obey all that He commanded. We are to teach believers how to be like Jesus and invite them to make disciples. We do this both by equipping them to know and obey the Word and by modeling a life of holiness, a community of love, and a mission of obedience. Here's the main idea:

> With a burden to see lives transformed and a world impacted by the gospel, we are committed to equip believers from the Word of God and model lives of discipline, obedience, and love.

Session Outline
- Equip
  - Short-Term Discipleship
  - Long-Term Discipleship
  - Obedience-Based Discipleship
- Model
  - Model Life
  - Model Community
  - Model Mission
- Assessing Church
  - The Early Church
  - Healthy Church
  - Time and Location

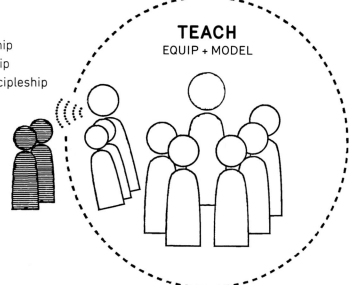

START

Welcome to this week's small-group study.

How are you?

How are you doing? How are we doing? What has God been teaching you?

How have you obeyed what we discussed last week?

Did you share the gospel with anyone this week? How did it go?

Worship + Parable Study

Spend some time worshipping God together in song.

Read Matthew 25:14-30, "The Talents."

What is the main message of this parable?

What does the parable tell us about how the kingdom grows?

What is our part?

What should we expect and how should you respond?

STUDY

Jesus told us to teach disciples to obey everything that He had commanded. And it is His desire to day by day bring change to your life and the lives of those you disciple. Paul writes to the Philippians, "And I am sure of this, that he who began a good work in you will bring it to completion at the day of Jesus Christ" (Philippians 1:6). He continues, "And it is my prayer that your love may abound more and more, with knowledge and all discernment, so that you may approve what is excellent, and so be pure and blameless for the day of Christ, filled with the fruit of righteousness that comes through Jesus Christ, to the glory and praise of God" (Philippians 1:9-11).

Equip

As we teach disciples, we need to keep in mind that everyone is at a different place in their journey. We should seek to understand where they are and how to best equip them for where they are going.

Short-Term Discipleship

The book of Hebrews identifies two groups of believers, both of which help us to better understand what we should teach. The first group is described as infants who must be fed with milk (Hebrews 5:12; see also 1 Corinthians 3:1-2; 1 Peter 2:2). The second is described as those who live on solid food.

Read Hebrews 5:12-6:3. How are believers who live on milk described?

What are the basic, or elementary, teachings mentioned?

What are some basic teachings that immature believers might need? Discuss and consider the following.

- **Salvation and the gospel:** Teach them about salvation and the gospel.
- **Bible Study:** Teach them how to read and study the Bible.
- **Worship:** Teach them how to grow in knowing and praising God.
- **Prayer:** Teach them how to pray.
- **Church:** Teach them how to grow in community with other believers.
- **Disciple Making:** Teach them how to make disciples.

- **Giving:** Teach them how to give to the church and those in need.
- **Baptism:** Teach them about obediently practicing baptism.
- **Lord's Supper:** Teach them about observing the Lord's Supper.
- **Persecution:** Prepare them for persecution.

Basic teachings such as these are often called short-term discipleship. It's short-term because these teachings provide the foundation a disciple needs to continue to grow long term as a healthy follower of Jesus.

Long-Term Discipleship

Discipleship is, and should be, an ongoing process of learning and transformation. Unlike the growth of a child, growing in faith is not measured by time but by maturity. As we go beyond equipping disciples in the fundamentals of the faith, we move toward touching every aspect of their lives with the Lordship of Jesus. Our role includes teaching them to grow to live on "solid food," correcting as necessary, and equipping for ministry and the building up of the church (see Ephesians 4:11-16). We call this long-term discipleship.

Read Hebrews 5:12-6:3. How are the believers who live on solid food described?

Sometimes you may be discipling people you have worked with since they began to follow Jesus. At other times, you may have the opportunity to come alongside and partner with existing believers, churches, or leaders. When you find or are connected with existing churches or believers, take time before getting too far along to personally get to know them and what they believe.

In considering the endless number of topics we could teach, we need to make sure that what we teach is biblically driven and focuses on how to be a disciple and how to make disciples. In the individuals and churches we have worked with, some areas where we have seen a need for further teaching include sharing the gospel, theology, strategy for engaging new areas, dating, marriage, parenting, stewardship, conflict resolution, and leadership. Another issue that frequently needs to be addressed cross-culturally is finding the sometimes blurry line where traditions and festivals begin to oppose God. With any of these topics, ask the Spirit to give you discernment and wisdom in how to address the issue using the Word. In all things, make sure to point others toward God and a gospel-centered life—a life marked by abiding in Christ, obeying His Word, and loving others.

Obedience-Based Discipleship

Are those you are teaching devoted to obediently following Jesus? Do they love God and others? Are they making disciples? As believers grow in maturity, with the help of the Spirit, they should begin to study and grow to obey the Word on their own, the evidence of which is real life transformation. From the beginning of discipleship, we should be careful to equip not only with knowledge but also with an expectation of devotion and obedience—what is sometimes called obedience-based discipleship.

Read Hebrews 6:10-12. How are obedient believers described?

Model

Authentic transformation happens in relationship—in relationship with Jesus, but also in relationship with other believers. Real discipleship includes not only equipping but also intentionally setting an example. We should help disciples go from where they are to where they could be—and, as we have opportunity, personally journeying with them.

Model Life

We can all too easily lose focus and get distracted. Life gets busy, and trials and temptations do come. Just thinking about the emotions, expectations, and busyness of investing in people's lives and making disciples, all while maintaining our own godliness, feels exhausting! But look at Paul's testimony as he urged the Philippians, "Brothers, join in imitating me, and keep your eyes on those who walk according to the example you have in us" (Philippians 3:17).

Read 1 Corinthians 11:1; 1 Thessalonians 1:6-7; 2 Timothy 2:2. Who were they to imitate?

Read Titus 2:7-8; 1 Timothy 4:12. What were they to model?

Are these qualities true of you? Can you say as Paul said, "Imitate me"? Are you that kind of person? Do you desire to be that kind of person? Are you keeping your eyes on faithful examples? We must personally examine whether we are truly living like this, but we also need—regardless of the season of life we are in—more mature believers to look to and mentor us.

How will you make sure you have people who are discipling you?

Model Community

Discipleship happens one-on-one, life-on-life, and also in community. This type of community makes the church. We are meant to join together—our common identity in Christ brings us together. As we seek to raise healthy, reproducing disciples we should regularly gather them for encouragement, instruction, and accountability. In community we have the opportunity, through the good and the bad, to commit to God and one another to obey all that Christ commanded. And we have the blessing to worship and study the Word as a body of believers. One place where we find instruction about how to function in this way is in Paul's letter to the church in Colossae.

Read Colossians 3:13-17. Who participates?

Read the following verses. How should believers in the church encourage each other?

Colossians 3:12

Colossians 3:13

Colossians 3:14

Colossians 3:15

Colossians 3:16

Read Colossians 1:28; 3:16. How should the church worship and study together?

Read the following verses. How should the church commit to obey?

Colossians 3:17

Colossians 3:23

Colossians 4:2

It is important to consider how to model the gathered church. In modeling a gospel-centered life and community, we need to be intentional about encouraging a culture of real disciple-ship that is personal and communal. Cultivate a place where everyone gets to participate and where everyone is being moved from where they are to where they could be.

Each of our sessions has been broken into thirds: start, study, and surrender. The instructions that Paul gave the Colossians, as well as the Ephesians, were to reach in, to reach up, and to reach out. These components, respectively, call for accountability and care, Bible teaching and worship, and commitment and prayer. A similar pattern is being used by many house churches around the world.[1]

As you pray about how you should model church, recognize that the structure in each culture and context may need to look different. For example, in Western and urban contexts, time may be a major constraint. If you can, plan for at least two hours, allowing 40 minutes for each part. If you only have one hour then schedule time for each third, always trying to retain each part. In other settings where time is not an issue, each component may blend into the other over the course of a few hours or a day. In these more fluid environments, don't force structure where it doesn't belong. Instead, regularly examine and evaluate—prayerfully crafting a process for that culture to ensure that everything that should take place does take place.

Discuss how to model the gathered church in your context by considering the suggestions below.

- **Reach In—Accountability and Care:** Encourage one another and help each other obey by asking intentional questions. How are you are doing? How are we doing? Any griev-ances? What has God been teaching you? What did we learn during our last meeting? How have you obeyed what we learned? Did you meet any new people? Did you share the gospel? What did you share? Did you teach anyone? How did it go? Pray over these things.

- **Reach Up—Bible Teaching and Worship:** Worship together in song. Open the Word together. Teach and learn from each other, always emphasizing that God's Word is our authority. The format used in the parable studies is one example of a simple Bible study method that is participative and meets the basic needs for long-term discipleship.
- **Reach Out—Commitment and Prayer:** Ask each other what you learned and how you need to obey. Commit and pray together.

Model Mission

Be what you are asking them to be, but also do what you are asking them to do. Model a gospel-centered life, community *and* mission. The pattern of disciple making should spread from one place to the next, one generation of believers to another. If you can, go with them to share the gospel and make disciples. Guide them in identifying the needs of the culture—encourage them to authentically engage and connect with the people of that culture. As you go, make sure that they know and can communicate the gospel. When you return, set aside time to debrief, to pray, and to set action plans for further engagement and follow-up. Assist them to the point where they can sustain their own life and mission through the power of the Spirit. And as they grow in their confidence and obedience, begin to step back and just watch. As the Spirit leads, be ready to follow Him to the next place that He has for you.[2]

Read 2 Corinthians 4:13-18. What did Paul teach the Corinthian church about making disciples?

Read Acts 18:1-18. What did Paul do and experience in Corinth?

Read 1 Corinthians 4:17. Where did Paul teach and model his way of life?

Assessing Church

As we equip believers, we want to help them stand on their own as a church. But this can be a challenge. The mission process will rarely be straightforward—along the way, we hope and pray the components that make a church will be picked up, but they don't necessarily all come together at the same time. The work may seem slow, and then opportunities arise that quickly move it forward. Other situations may force you to back up. You may have varying degrees of work going on in each step in the harvest, each at a different place with different strengths, weaknesses, and issues. At some point, maybe frequently, you need to assess what has taken shape. Then, if and when you find issues, lovingly and biblically address them.

The Early Church
Read Acts 2:38-47. Discuss the characteristics in this example of the early church.

Healthy Church

Even if a gathering of believers genuinely follow Jesus and only Jesus, a question of whether or not they are a church may remain. The question is undoubtedly important, but the answer can be hard to agree on. It may be helpful to develop a working definition of church to try to assess the health of the believers and their functioning together as a church.

Read the verses below. Discuss how these passages relate to building a healthy church.[3]

Hebrews 10:24-25

1 Timothy 4:13

2 Timothy 4:1-2

Ephesians 5:19; Colossians 3:16

Philippians 4:6; Colossians 4:2; James 5:13-16

Matthew 28:19; Acts 2:41; Romans 6:3-5

1 Corinthians 11:23-26

Matthew 18:15-17; 1 Corinthians 11:27-32

Colossians 3:12-15

Titus 1:5-8; 1 Timothy 3:1-13

Acts 20:35; 2 Corinthians 9:6-7; Galatians 6:6-10

Acts 1:8

Time and Location

Though the church is instructed to meet together regularly, there is no command for when to meet. Historically, many churches have met at least once per week, typically on Sunday.[4] Today, for a variety of cultural and economic reasons, many churches around the world find other weekly meeting times that better enable them to gather together. Another component not clearly prescribed in the Bible is the type of location(s) where churches should meet.

Read Acts 2:46; 5:42; Romans 16:5. Where did the early church meet?

The early church was typically known to meet in both public and private spaces. Different lo-cations have different advantages or disadvantages depending on the context. Churches may meet in a building they own or rent or in a place such as a home, school, office space, coffee shop, tent, park, or theater. When money is scarce or persecution is high, they may meet in places like fields or caves.

At times, it can be hard to know if certain characteristics are truly essential for a group to be called a church. You need to come up with a basic working definition of what church is that is based on what the Bible teaches with consideration given to what you understand about your people group.[5] Use your definition and list of characteristics to decide if the groups you work with meet the qualifications to be called a church. If they do meet the basic qualifications, then examine whether they are a healthy church. The difference between a church and a healthy church is something you should start examining now—if you haven't already. I encourage you to check out the many great resources and courses available for studying about the church in greater depth. In every situation, prayerfully consider how you can build up the churches you are working with.[6]

If transformation stops after conversion, they weren't converted. If it stops after instruction, according to Paul they get puffed up. They may be able to answer all kinds of Bible questions, understand theology, and even write inspirational books, but they'll never know Christ on an intimate level that leads to true transformation. Only the person who converges the two—what they learn on a consistent basis with their lifestyle—has any hope of transformation.

—BOB ROBERTS JR., TRANSFORMATION[7]

SURRENDER

Review
Use the following questions to briefly review the content of this week's study.

What is discipleship? What is good discipleship?

How are we to equip—and who do we equip—with short-term discipleship? With long-term discipleship? With obedience-based discipleship?

How should we model a godly life?

How should we model community?

How should we model our mission?

What is church? What is a healthy church?

Response + Prayer
In groups of two or three, discuss the following questions.

Do you regularly examine your life and your teaching?

How are you doing as a disciple of Jesus? How are you being discipled?

What do you think church should look like in your community?

What about the people group you are going to serve?

What did you take away from this week's study? What will you do in response?

What prayer requests do you have?

How can we pray for our community?

How can we pray for the people we are going to serve?

Spend some time praying for each other.

PLAN: TEACH

WHERE ARE YOU AT?

Are you making disciples who make disciples? Explain.

List the methods and materials commonly being used for short-term discipleship with people groups similar to the one that you are serving.

WHERE ARE YOU GOING?

Circle the discipleship method above that you will use for short-term discipleship. Write a goal for how you will equip believers.

What will you do for long-term discipleship?

Where will you meet for discipleship? When will you meet?

What will discipleship groups do when they meet together? Write out a simple form of church.

How will you create a culture in your groups that includes accountability and care?

What will you need to be intentional about in order to model being a disciple and making disciples? Write a goal for the areas that you need to focus on this year as you make disciples.

REMOTE UNENGAGED VILLAGE.

REACH: LEAD + MULTIPLY

I will make you as a light for the nations, that my salvation may reach to the end of the earth. ISAIAH 49:6B

In this session, we will learn about how the harvest multiplies (Mark 4:8, 20). In the Great Commission, Jesus commands us to "make disciples of *all* nations" (Matthew 28:19a, emphasis mine). Paul understood this as he saturated groups of people and areas with the gospel. And we look forward to the fulfillment of John's vision when, one day, there will be "a great multitude that no one [can] number, from every nation, from all tribes and peoples and languages, standing before the throne and before the Lamb" (Revelation 7:9b). We pray for and expect movements that result in a saturation of the gospel in both geography and people group affinity that in turn results in disciples who make disciples and churches who plant churches. Here's the main idea:

> We are intentional in our efforts to raise leaders and to plant biblically healthy, multiplying disciples and churches with a vision to be a light for the nations that reaches to the end of the earth.

Session Outline
- Lead
  - Choosing Leaders
  - Qualifications for Leadership
- Multiply
- Gospel-Centered Life on a Gospel-Centered Mission

REACH
LEAD + MULTIPLY

START

Welcome to this week's small-group session.

How are you?

How are you doing? How are we doing? What has God been teaching you?

How have you obeyed what we discussed last week?

Did you share the gospel with anyone this week? How did it go?

Worship + Parable Study

Spend some time worshipping God together in song.

Read Mark 4:26-29, "The Growing Seed."

What is the main message of this parable?

What does the parable tell us about how the kingdom grows?

What is our part?

What should we expect and how should you respond?

STUDY

Short-term overseas trips and increased time in the Word stirred a passion for international missions in me as a college student. I earnestly sought to make the most of the opportunities I had at my university, but I never made a deep connection with an international student—despite my efforts and prayers. Then, the semester after I graduated, I met Tim.[1] Tim was a graduate student from Asia, and we had a lot in common. But I soon learned that due to bad experiences with other believers, Tim had put a number of walls up. A few weeks later, after dinner at my house, I felt compelled to ask him if he'd like to study the Bible with me.

Tim showed interest in frequently wanting to study the Word together, but at the same time it was hard to know whether he was growing more attracted or more resistant to Jesus. At one point he expressed his struggle, "To believe this means that everything I have believed before is a lie." Amazingly, at the same time that Tim was struggling with the gospel, he was sharing it with his older brother, Paul, back in Asia. One word described Paul's response: militant. But Tim kept studying, kept struggling, and kept growing closer to Jesus. After about six months, Tim began to follow Jesus.

My wife and I later moved to the country where Paul lived. A combination of natural disasters and political instability had us temporarily relocated to the city where he and his wife lived. The first night that he heard we were in town, he came straight to meet us. He knew we had only been studying his language for about a year at that time, but he still hit us with what felt like a million questions. I didn't know if we were being interrogated or making a friend—but Paul was persistent, and we did our best to answer him with wisdom, honesty, and love. Each night that week our conversation continued. One part of me thought there was no way that this guy would ever believe—but the other part was hopeful that it was the same pattern I had seen years before with his brother Tim. The following week, Paul was different. He resembled the same person, but at the same time he didn't. I asked him if he had become a follower of Jesus, and he immediately responded with a big grin and an emphatic "Yes!"

Over the next few years we were able to arrange regular trips back to visit Paul and his wife. They continued to grow more and more in their relationship with Jesus, and they quickly became involved in an underground house church. Eventually we were able to introduce a trusted friend and colleague to Paul. We've since heard amazing reports that Paul has become a bold leader in his church and in mobilizing disciples to other unreached areas. The story of how an international student's faith spread back to his brother in Asia and has since impacted an Asian megacity and beyond is one of those things many of us pray and hope for but rarely get to see.

It has been a blessing for us to have a small part in this story. And it has served as a constant reminder of the power of the Spirit and the message of the gospel to reach beyond what we ever imagine, multiplying from one person and one community to another.

Lead

Seeing growth in believers and the formation of discipleship groups is exciting. Regardless of the challenges we sometimes face, teaching a new generation of believers should bring us a deep sense of joy. But this isn't the end. We need to remind ourselves where we are headed. We need to ask what our end goal is. It is the Father's plan that Jesus' mission be continued and reproduced through His followers. The groups that have formed, or that we have partnered with, should be given the opportunity to take leadership in making disciples and teaching. And they should be invited to take part in continuing the mission of the church.

Read the following verses. What needs to happen to see groups of believers take ownership in making disciples?

Acts 13:1-3

Acts 14:23

Titus 1:5

Choosing Leaders

Each situation is going to have a different set of factors for finding and raising up local leaders. The first step is identifying who to invest in. The move from outsider-led discipleship group to locally led church may or may not be a natural or easy transition. With existing churches and leaders, it may take time to get them on course and make any necessary corrections. At times that may be easy. In some circumstances, you may have qualified men, such as Paul describes, who "[aspire] to the office of overseer" (1 Timothy 3:1b). At other times, the search for such leaders might be long and hard. In the Gospels, we can observe how Jesus chose leaders.[2]

Read Luke 5:1-2, 15. At the broadest scale, who was interested in Jesus?

Read Luke 6:12-16. How many disciples did He have? Whom did Jesus choose?

Read Luke 8:49-56; 9:28-36; Mark 14:32-33. Who was in Jesus' core inner circle?

Jesus' fame quickly spread. As more and more people heard about Him, great crowds came to hear Him and to be healed. Quickly, a tribe of followers formed from within the throngs of people that came. But Jesus didn't focus on everyone. He prayerfully chose 12 apostles from this tribe to spend most of His time with. And there were three He especially focused on: Peter, James, and John.

Qualifications for Leadership

Knowing how to choose leaders is one thing. But knowing who to choose as a leader is another. There are certain characteristics that will either qualify or disqualify a believer for leadership. These foundational qualifications for leadership have to do with the character and reputation of the person. Then there are other factors to consider that have to do with the quality of leadership. Our role in finding qualified leaders and raising up quality leaders is important to consider and understand.

Read Ephesians 4:11-16. What are the leaders of the church given to do?

Read 2 Timothy 2:2. What kind of disciple maker are they to be?

Read 1 Peter 5:1-3. How should they lead?

Titus 1:6-9; 2:1-15; 1Timothy 3:1-13. What are the qualifications for local leadership?

Some leaders may be capable and ready to lead early on, but many will require a mentor to come alongside to help them for a season. Whenever the circumstances allow, assist and encourage these new leaders. Then as they gain the skills and confidence they need, slowly pull back until they are ready to be released to stand on their own.

Multiply

With His parting words, Jesus told His disciples they would receive the power of the Holy Spirit and would be His witnesses from Jerusalem to the ends of the earth (Acts 1:8). When Jesus had earlier promised the Holy Spirit, He also told them that "in that day you will know that I am in my Father, and you in me, and I in you" (John 14:20). As we go to make disciples, we must remain in Him. Using the simple illustration of a vine, Jesus explained that only by remaining in Him would His disciples bear fruit (John 15:5). True disciples of Jesus are known by the good fruit that they bear—our lives should clearly show that we are followers of Jesus.

Paul's faithfulness and obedience to live for Christ, preach the gospel, and teach disciples led to the formation of multiple generations of believers and churches. During his third missionary journey, Paul's teaching in Ephesus spread "so that all the residents of Asia heard the word of the Lord" (Acts 19:10). From there he wrote to the church at Corinth, urging them to imitate him and reminding them of his way of life, which reflected what he taught "everywhere in every church" (1 Corinthians 4:16-17; see also 11:1). And from prison Paul wrote Timothy, who was serving in Ephesus at the time, encouraging him to "be strengthened by the grace that is in Christ Jesus," and instructing him to "entrust to faithful men who will be able to teach others" the teaching he received from Paul (2 Timothy 2:1-2). This short statement in 2 Timothy 2 is commonly understood as an instruction to pass on sound teaching to a minimum of four generations—Paul to Timothy, Timothy to faithful believers, and faithful believers to other faithful believers. To see how this plays out, I've found it helpful to back up the timeline and look at the example in Thessalonica.

During Paul's second missionary journey, he and his companions stopped in Thessalonica in the province of Macedonia for three Sabbaths, or three to four weeks (Acts 17:1-4). A number of people there were persuaded to follow Jesus, but some of the Jews became jealous and formed a mob. The believers in Thessalonica quickly responded by sending Paul and Silas down the road to the town of Berea. There the people "received the word with all eagerness, examining the Scriptures daily," and many of them believed (Acts 17:11-12). But Luke goes on to report that when the Jews from Thessalonica heard this, they went to Berea to stir up more trouble. Silas and Timothy stayed behind, but Paul was sent off by way of sea. From there, Paul continued south through Athens and settled in the city of Corinth, in the province of Achaia, where he served for 18 months. Timothy later joined Paul in Corinth, bringing with him a report about the church in Thessalonica:

> But now that Timothy has come to us from you, and has brought us the good news of your faith and love and reported that you always remember us kindly and long to see us, as we long to see you—for this reason, brothers, in all our distress and affliction we have been comforted about you through your faith. (1 Thessalonians 3:6-7)

With all that had taken place, their faithfulness had to have been an incredible encouragement to Paul. But what is also interesting to take note of is how we can clearly trace in this letter how the gospel spread through these faithful believers to other faithful believers, spanning two provinces and beyond (1 Thessalonians 1:6-8).

Read 1 Thessalonians 1:1-8. Draw arrows to show who imitated whom and discuss how believers and churches multiplied.

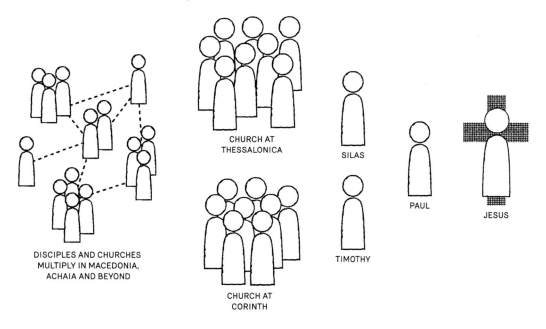

DISCIPLES AND CHURCHES
MULTIPLY IN MACEDONIA,
ACHAIA AND BEYOND

CHURCH AT
THESSALONICA

CHURCH AT
CORINTH

SILAS

TIMOTHY

PAUL

JESUS

The story of the early church continued as disciples multiplied and were added to the church. The gospel spread and saturated both geography and people group affinities. And the growing number of disciples gathered into churches, which provided necessary discipleship for the new and maturing followers of Jesus. This multiplicative pattern that began then continues today—it is reaching further and further as new generations of believers grow in imitating Jesus and faithful examples of Him.

Read 1 Thessalonians 2:11-12. How will you create an environment where disciples make disciples who make disciples?

Your passion for the Lord and burden for the lost can be very contagious. Make the most of every opportunity to share a vision of increasing numbers of people knowing and worshipping Jesus. And invite and empower other believers through ongoing discipleship to take the gospel to those who are unreached.

Teach and model for other believers how to be a disciple. Provide them with clear and humble direction for how to identify needs and genuinely connect with people as they *go and make disciples*. Teach them to expect the working of the Spirit and how to share their faith as they *preach the gospel*. Teach them to equip in short-term, long-term, and obedience-based discipleship, and encourage them to model a life of holiness, a community of love, and a mission of obedience as they *teach the gospel*. Teach them to raise biblically qualified and healthy leaders who are empowered to multiply and *reach others with the gospel*. All of these things start with simple and active steps of faith and obedience.

Gospel-Centered Life on a Gospel-Centered Mission

Studying church-planting strategy is good. It is important. Talking about best strategies, best tools, and best practices can no doubt be helpful. But with this mission it is imperative that with all that can be said about *making* disciples, we also understand what it means to *be* a disciple. We must seek after one thing: to know and worship the One who is sending us. This is as much about being as it is about doing.

Read the verses below. What type of person does God desire you to be? What does this need to look like in your relationships, church, ministry, and partnerships?

Proverbs 3:1-12

Proverbs 10:8-19

Proverbs 18:9-15

Proverbs 27:1-5

Proverbs 27:17-19

In cooperation with the sending Father, sent Son, and commissioning Holy Spirit, we join our prayers to yours: that every member contains within them a church, and every church contains within her a movement. We are standing at a pivot point in history. We are on the verge.

—DAVE FERGUSON AND ALAN HIRSH, *ON THE VERGE*[3]

SURRENDER

Review
Use the following questions to briefly review the content of this week's study.

How do we choose leaders?

What are the biblical qualifications for leadership?

How might disciples multiply across your community? What about the people group you are going to serve?

What type of person does God desire you to be? What does this need to look like in your relationships, church, ministry, and partnerships?

Response + Prayer
In groups of two or three, discuss the following questions.

In terms of making disciples and planting churches, what do you hope to see happen?

What is your plan for making disciples in your community? What about the people group you are going to serve?

What did you take away from this week's study? What will you do in response?

What prayer requests do you have?

How can we pray for our community?

How can we pray for the people we are going to serve?

Spend some time praying together.

Spend some time praying together.

YOUR PLAN: REACH

WHERE ARE YOU AT?

Who are the national and/or local partners you are working with? List their names.

Think about how each of the people above is doing as a disciple and a disciple maker. Circle the top two or three people you will invest in (this may not be contingent on whether you assess them as doing well or not).

Who do you recognize as potential new leaders? List their names.

Circle the people above who you perceive to be open to receive leadership training. How will you mentor, disciple, and train these potential new leaders?

Who are the churches you partner with back home and around the world? How will they each be a part of the work?

WHERE ARE YOU GOING?

How will you share your vision with others?

What is your plan for making disciples among your people group(s)? Can you share it with local partners and with churches back home? Can you share your plan in under five minutes? Can you illustrate it simply on a page? Can you share it in more detail? Use a separate document to write out your plan and develop a clear way to communicate it with others.

How will you develop leaders to make disciples who make disciples? What will you teach? How often and for how long will you have concentrated times of training? How will you set action plans and follow-up with them?

How will you encourage and equip leaders to split and launch new generations of churches?

RECOMMENDED READING

If you would like to explore further the topics in this book or find evangelism and discipleship tools, then I recommend the following resources. Though I recommend these and have found them helpful, I do not necessarily agree with everything in them.

MISSION STRATEGY

Addison, Steve. *Movements that Change the World: Five Keys to Spreading the Gospel* (Downers Grove, IL: IVP Books, 2011).

Addison, Steve. *What Jesus Started: Joining the Movement, Changing the World* (Downers Grove, IL: IVP Books, 2012).

Chan, Francis, and Mark Beuving. *Multiply: Disciples Making Disciples* (Colorado Springs, CO: David C. Cook, 2012).

DeYoung, Kevin, and Greg Gilbert. *What Is the Mission of the Church? Making Sense of Social Justice, Shalom, and the Great Commission* (Wheaton, IL: Crossway, 2011).

Fielding, Charles. *Preach and Heal: A Biblical Model for Mission* (Richmond, VA: International Mission Board, 2008).

Hirsh, Alan. *The Forgotten Ways: Reactivating the Missional Church* (Grand Rapids, MI: Brazos Press, 2006).

McCrary, Larry, Caleb Crider, Wade Stephens, and Rodney Calfee. *Tradecraft: For the Church on Mission* (Portland, OR: Urban Loft Publishers, 2013).

Piper, John, and David Mathis, ed. *Finish the Mission: Bringing the Gospel to the Unreached and Unengaged* (Wheaton, IL: Crossway, 2012).

Putman, Jim, and Bobby Harrington. *Discipleshift: Five Steps that Help Your Church to Make Disciples Who Make Disciples* (Grand Rapids, MI: Zondervan, 2013).

Smith, Steve, with Ying Kai. *T4T: A Discipleship ReRevolution* (Monument, CO: WIGTake Resources, 2011).

Stetzer, Ed. *Sent: Living the Missional Nature of the Church* (Nashville, TN: LifeWay Press, 2008).

Terry, John Mark and J.D. Payne. *Developing a Strategy for Missions: A Biblical, Historical, and Cultural Introduction* (Grand Rapids, MI: Baker Academic, 2013).

PERSONAL GROWTH

Bridges, Jerry. *The Pursuit of Holiness* (Colorado Springs, CO: NavPress, 1978).

Bridges, Jerry. *True Community: The Biblical Practice of Koinonia* (Colorado Springs, CO: NavPress, 2012).

Carroll, Joseph S. *How to Worship Jesus Christ* (Chicago, IL: Moody Publishers, 1991).

Chan, Francis, with Danae Yankoski. *Forgotten God: Reversing Our Tragic Neglect of the Holy Spirit* (Colorado Springs, CO: David C. Cook, 2009).

Chandler, Matt, with Jared Wilson. *The Explicit Gospel* (Wheaton, IL: Crossway, 2012).

Cloud, Henry, and John Townsend. *Boundaries: When to Say Yes, How to Say No to Take Control of Your Life* (Grand Rapids, MI: Zondervan, 1992).

Cloud, Henry, and John Townsend. *How to Have That Difficult Conversation You've Been Avoiding* (Grand Rapids, MI: Zondervan, 2003).

Cordeiro, Wayne, with Francis Chan and Larry Osborne. *Sifted: Pursuing Growth through Trials, Challenges, and Disappointments* (Grand Rapids, MI: Zondervan, 2012).

DeYoung, Kevin. *Just Do Something: A Liberating Approach to Finding God's Will* (Chicago, IL: Moody Publishers, 2009).

DeYoung, Kevin. *The Hole in Our Holiness: Filling the Gap between Gospel Passion and the Pursuit of Godliness* (Wheaton, IL: Crossway, 2012).

Hoover, Christine. *The Church Planting Wife: Help and Hope for Her Heart* (Chicago, IL: Moody Publishers, 2013).

Miller, Paul. *A Praying Life: Connecting with God in a Distracting World* (Colorado Springs, CO: NavPress, 2009).

Murray, Andrew. *Absolute Surrender* (Chicago, IL: Moody Press, 1895).

Piper, John. *Desiring God: Meditations of a Christian Hedonist* (Sisters, OR: Multnomah, 2003).

Piper, John. *Let the Nations Be Glad!: The Supremacy of God in Missions*, Third Edition (Grand Rapids, MI: Baker Academic, 2010).

Platt, David. *Follow Me: A Call to Die. A Call to Live.* (Carol Stream, IL: Tyndale House Publishers, 2013).

Rankin, Jerry. *Spiritual Warfare: The Battle for God's Glory* (Nashville, TN: B&H Publishing, 2009).

Stetzer, Ed, and Philip Nation. *Compelled: Living the Mission of God* (Birmingham, AL: New Hope Publishers, 2012).

Swensen, Richard A. *In Search of Balance: Keys to a Stable Life* (Colorado Springs, CO: NavPress, 2010).

TerKeurst, Lysa. *Made to Crave: Satisfying Your Deepest Desire with God, Not Food* (Grand Rapids, MI: Zondervan, 2010).

Tozer, A.W. *The Knowledge of the Holy* (San Francisco, CA: HarperSanFrancisco, 1961).

EVANGELISM

Creation to Christ (C2C). Accessible at http://c2cstory.com/story/

Cross, John R. *The Stranger on the Road to Emmaus* (Canada: GoodSeed·International, 2011). This book and other adaptations available at http://www.goodseed.com/

Dever, Mark. *The Gospel and Personal Evangelism* (Wheaton, IL: Crossway, 2007).

"Experiencing God's Grace" (Louisville, KY: The Southern Baptist Theological Seminary, 2009). Available at https://www.bkstr.com/ProductDisplay/10001-10062-201405-4000000000002380791-1?demoKey=d

Hovind, Chad. *Fast Track: Genesis to Revelation: The Quickest Way to Understand the Bible* (Nashville, TN: LifeWay Press, 2013).

Jesus Film (Orlando, FL: Campus Crusade for Christ), video. Viewable at http://jesusfilmmedia.org/video/1_529-jf-0-0/english/jesus

J.O. Terry's Bible Storying Resources.

Metzger, Will. *Tell the Truth: The Whole Gospel Wholly by Grace Communicated Truthfully & Lovingly*, Fourth Edition (Downers Grove, IL: InterVarsity Press, 2012).

McIlwain, Trevor. *Building on Firm Foundations, Revised Edition* (Sanford, FL: New Tribes Mission, 2005). Available at http://www.ntmbooks.com/chronological_teaching
Accompanying Bible pictures available at http://www.ntmbooks.com/bible_pictures_1

One Story Media. Accessible at http://www.onestory-media.org/

Orality Strategies. Accessible at https://orality.imb.org/strategies/

OT & NT Bible Story Picture Card Decks. Learn more at http://www.123goshare.com/

Packer, J.I. *Evangelism and the Sovereignty of God* (Downers Grove, IL: IVP Press, 2008).

Perry, Bill. *Storyteller's Bible Study, Second Edition* (Ephrata, PA: Multi-Language Media). Available at http://www.multilanguage.com/feature.htm

Shipman, Mike. *Any-3: Anyone, Anywhere, Anytime.* (Monument, CO: WIGTake Resources, 2013).

Stiles, J. Mack. *Marks of the Messenger: Knowing, Living and Speaking the Gospel* (Downers Grover, IL: InterVarsity Press, 2010).

The God's Stories (GRC Productions), video series. Viewable at http://www.godsstories.com/en/

The Hope: The Story of God's Promise for All People (Missouri City, TX: Mars-Hill Productions), DVD, (2002). Viewable at http://www.thehopeproject.com/

"The Prophets Story." (Antioch, TX), video. Viewable at http://theprophetsstory.com/

The Story (Bloomington, IL: Spread Truth Publishing, 2012). Learn more at http://viewthestory.com/

Warren, Barry. *Perspective: Spiritual Conversation Cards* (Orlando, FL: CruPress, 2011). Learn more at http://www.perspectivecards.com/

DISCIPLESHIP

Chan, Francis and Mark Beuving. *Multiply: Disciples Making Disciples* (Colorado Springs, CO: David C Cook, 2012). Learn more at http://www.multiplymovement.com

Cross, John R. *The Stranger on the Road to Emmaus* (Canada: GoodSeed International, 2011).

Dever, Mark. *The Church: The Gospel Made Visible* (Nashville, TN: B&H Publishing Group, 2012).

Grudem, Wayne. *Christian Beliefs: Twenty Basics Every Christian Should Know* (Grand Rapids, MI: Zondervan, 2011).

Jameson, Bobbie. *Sound Doctrine: How a Church Grows in Love and Holiness of God* (Wheaton, IL: Crossway, 2013).

Plummer, Robert L. *40 Questions About Interpreting the Bible* (Grand Rapids, MI: Kregel Publications, 2010).

"Secret Church." Radical. Accessible at http://www.radical.net/media/schurch/

The Gospel Project Series. (Nashville, TN: LifeWay Press, 2012).

LEADERSHIP

Anyabwile, Thabiti M. *Finding Faithful Elders and Deacons* (Wheaton, IL: Crossway, 2012).

Coleman, Robert E. *The Master Plan of Evangelism* (Grand Rapids, MI: Revell, 1963).

Fernando, Ajith. *Jesus Driven Ministry* (Wheaton, IL: Crossway Books, 2002).

Iorg, Jeff. *The Character of Leadership: Nine Qualities that Define Great Leaders* (Nashville, TN: B&H Publishing Group, 2007).

Mohler, Albert. *The Conviction to Lead: 25 Principles for Leadership that Matters* (Bloomington, MN: Bethany House Publishers, 2012).

Payne, J.D. *Roland Allen: Pioneer of Spontaneous Expansion* (J.D. Payne, 2012).

Sanders, J Oswald. *Spiritual Leadership* (Chicago, IL: Moody Publishers, 1967).

ENDNOTES

Introduction

1. When I was a sophomore in college, my Dad handed me Joseph Carroll's book *How to Worship Jesus Christ*—it forever changed my outlook on life and my relationship with Jesus. The first chapter of Carroll's book, titled "One Thing Needful," is the inspiration for the theme and title of this book. Joseph Carroll, *How to Worship Jesus Christ*, Moody Publishers Edition, 1991 (Chicago, IL: Moody Publishers, 1991), Chapter 1 "One Thing Needful", Kindle.

2. J.C. Ryle, *Practical Religion* (London: William Hunt and Company, 1883), Chapter 8 "Christian Zeal," Kindle.

How to Use this Study

1. The Small-Group Study version of *One Thing* was adapted at the request of and with input provided by Debbie Stephens, president and founder of Equipped to Go and leader of Jet Set with the Upstream Collective, and Chad Stillwell, IMB Student Mobilization.

Session 1: Gospel-Centered Life

1. The parable study was adapted from a component of Hands On orientation by Jacob Franklin. The Facilitator Guide in the complete *One Thing* also provides examples for how to adapt these questions for the study of almost any Bible passage. The questions for the parable study are not entirely original—the two Bible study methods that I primarily considered were the "SOS" method found in Steve Smith and Ying Kai's *T4T: A Discipleship ReRevolution* (Monument, CO: WIGTake Resources, 2011), "Chapter 7: The Three-Thirds Process" under "Part 5: New Lessons (or Bible Study);" and the "Sword Bible Study Method," accessed January 12, 2014, http://www.movements.net/2012/03/24/seven-stories-of-hope-1-the-sinful-woman.html

2. My inspiration in using Isaiah 6 was from a sermon by Francis Chan, Smoky Mountain Winterfest Conference, March 11, 2011; after teaching this content for a couple of years with local partners, Clive Cowell, a friend and former executive director of the Bible Institute of Hawaii, reviewed and provided valuable feedback for this session.

3. The term "absolute surrender" comes from Andrew Murray's book, Absolute Surrender (Chicago, IL: The Moody Publishers, 1897).

4. This paragraph is a retelling of the story found in Acts 1:12-2:47.

5. See John 14:12 and comments made in Session 1 under "The Helper" for the first instance; the second is John 15:7; and the third is John 16:23-24.

6. Much insight for this chapter was gleaned from Paul Miller's "What Do We Do with Jesus' Extravagant Promise about Prayer," *A Praying Life: Connecting with God in a Distracting World* (Colorado Springs, CO: NavPress, 2009), Kindle.

7. Paul's example of prayer: Read the passages below and categorize Paul's prayer life and teaching on prayer as follows. In the first column, put the Scripture reference. In the second column, write when he prayed. In the third column, write where he prayed. In the final

column, write what he prayed *for*, what he *asked* prayer for, what he *taught* about prayer, and what he *thanked* God for in prayer—for the latter three categories, write ASK, TAUUGHT, or THANKED at the beginning of the column. When I did this study, I found it helpful to arrange the passages by approximate chronological order. First Journey: Acts 14:23. Second Journey: Acts 16:25; 1 Thessalonians 3:10; 5:17, 25; 2 Thessalonians 1:11-12; 3:1-2. Third Journey: 1 Corinthians 1:4-9; 14:15; 2 Corinthians 1:11; 13:7, 9; Romans 1:8-10; 8:26; 10:1; 12:12; 15:30-33; Acts 20:36-38; 21:5; 22:17. In transit to Rome: Acts 28:8. In house arrest in Rome: Ephesians 1:15-22; 3:14-21; 6:18; Philippians 1:3-11, 19; 4:6; Colossians 1:9-12; 4:2-3. After release from house arrest: 1 Timothy 2:1; 2:8. In prison in Rome before martyrdom: 2 Timothy 1:3.

8. Francis Chan, *Forgotten God: Reversing Our Tragic Neglect of the Holy Spirit* (Colorado Springs, CO: David C. Cook, 2009), Under Chapter 7 "Supernatural Church" under "Forceful or Forced?" Kindle.

Session 2: Abide

1. Andrew Murray, *Absolute Surrender*, Chapter 1 "Absolute Surrender," Kindle.

Session 3: Obey

1. For further study on trials and persecution, read and study the following. 1) Promised: John 15:18-25; 16:33; Romans 8:16-17; Philippians 1:29; 2 Timothy 3:12; 1 Peter 2:20-21. 2) Purpose: Romans 8:17-18, 28; Philippians 3:7-11; Hebrews 12:10b; 1 Peter 1:6-7. 3) Perseverance: Romans 5:3-5; James 5:10-11. 4) Privilege: Matthew 5:10-12; 1 Peter 3:14a; 4:13-14. 5) Permitted: 1 Peter 5:8-11.

2. The influence for writing, "not because you must or should but because you *want* to" comes from Lysa TerKeurst, *Made to Crave: Satisfying Your Deepest Desire with God, Not Food* (Grand Rapids, MI: Zondervan, 2010), 11, Kindle.

3. Amy Carmichael, *Things As They Are: Mission Work in Southern India* (A Public Domain Book), End of Chapter 18 "The Call Intensified," Kindle.

Session 4: Love

1. Details obscured to protect the identity of those individuals connected to this story.

2. For further study on the common identity we share, see the following verses. For "One Body," see also Romans 12:4-8; 1 Corinthians 12:12-27; Ephesians 4:15-16; Colossians 3:15. For "One Spirit," see also 1 Corinthians 12:4-13; Ephesians 2:18. For "One Hope," see also Hebrews 10:23-24. For "One Lord," see also Deuteronomy 6:4-5; Zechariah 14:9; 1 Corinthians 8:4-6. For "One Faith," see also Romans 3:22-24. For "One Baptism," see also Romans 6:3-4. For "One God," see also 1 John 4:4. For "One Father," see also Matthew 12:48-50.

3. I recommend books by Henry Cloud and John Townsend including Boundaries and *How to Have That Difficult Conversation You've Been Avoiding* (complete bibliographical information in "Recommended Resources").

4. Jerry Bridges, *True Community: The Biblical Practice of Koinonia* (Colorado Springs, CO: NavPress, 2012), Chapter 6 "Partnership in the Gospel," Kindle.

SECTION 2 INTRODUCTION

1. I was first introduced to a similar model by Ryan Parker in his training *God's Farming: The 5 Parts of Church Planting* (Kathmandu: J. Ryan Parker, 2010). This training uses the metaphor of a farmer to communicate the church-planting process to rural people groups. Another similar model that I compared was "'Four Fields of Kingdom Growth:' A Manual for Church Planting Facilitation: Starting and Releasing Healthy Churches, 2007," compiled by Nathan and Kari Shank, Accessed April 23, 2013, http://www.churchplantingmovements.com/images/stories/pdf/4_Fields_Final_Oct_2014.pdf. In addition, I had the opportunity to attend Steve Addison's "Movements" training at First Baptist Concord's Kingdom Impact Conference October 10-14, 2012, where Steve taught the model presented in his book, *What Jesus Started: Joining the Movement, Changing the World* (Downers Grove, IL: IVP Books, 2012).

2. In our original model, we referred to "four harvest fields." My editor, Mary Jane Welch, made a significant contribution to the communication of this model by changing the wording to "steps in the harvest."

3. The "preach" step in the harvest model of this study refers to evangelism.

Session 5: Gospel-Centered Mission

1. Jackson Wu and Andy Pettigrew provided valuable critique and input to the early versions of this session.

2. The topic of the gospel has been highly debated, discussed, and written about by many in recent years. Much of what has been said and written was taken into account in the development of the four questions used in this session. Others such as Greg Gilbert and Bobbie Jameson (complete bibliographical information in "Recommended Resources") have defined the gospel with a similar outline. The most influential resource in the final presentation of the gospel in this session was the four main parts: Creation, Fall, Rescue, Restoration from *The Story*, Spread Truth Ministries, Accessed August 5, 2013, http://viewthestory.com/.

3. Thom Wolf's teaching on "The Universal Disciple Pattern" was my main inspiration for using Ephesians as a contextualization model for communicating the gospel. Thom Wolf. "The Universal Disciple Pattern," University Institute educational edition 2000, Accessed April 23, 2013, http://www.scribd.com/doc/6775326/The-Universal-Discipleship-Pattern

4. See Isaiah 6 and refer to the section "Absolute Surrender" in Session 1 "Gospel-Centered Life."

5. "Drawing the Net" in Session 7 "Preach: Expect + Share" will provide more study and discussion regarding what is included in calling the lost to respond.

6. We intentionally do not offer a definition of the gospel in this session. Our purpose is to drive participants, in the accountability of community, to seek a clear, biblical definition of the gospel by prayerfully studying the Bible, internalizing its message, and putting it into practice. We believe the gospel to be the good news of salvation by Jesus Christ and have adopted the *Baptist Faith and Message 2000* definition of salvation (Accessible at http://www.sbc.net/bfm2000/bfm2000.asp).

Session 6: Go

1. Phil Nelson, while serving as missions pastor at First Baptist Concord, came up with "community, country, continents" as a way of communicating "Jerusalem, and in all Judea and Samaria, and to the end of the earth" (Acts 1:8).
2. Some versions refer to 70 sent ones rather than 72. As the *English Standard Version* has been used as the primary version for this book, we have chosen to use 72 in accordance with that translation.
3. Ed Stetzer and Philip Nation, *Compelled: Living the Mission of God* (Birmingham, AL: New Hope Publishers, 2012), 61, Kindle.

Session 7: Preach

1. Though I use the *Global Status of Evangelical Christianity* map to point out my own criticalness, it remains a helpful tool for understanding global trends of lostness. The most recent map can be accessed at http://public.imb.org/globalresearch/Pages/MapProgress.aspx.
2. I borrowed the idea of "identifying the harvest" from Pastor Scott Cagle of North Star Church in Knoxville, TN. I have heard Pastor Scott teach and talk of looking for the low hanging fruit and going after it.
3. Jeff Walters of The Southern Baptist Theological Seminary taught Five Fs that include "Food, Family, Festivals, Friends, Future/Faith." This was shared by two participants during the second piloting of *One Thing* and then adapted to the content being taught in this session.
4. See also Mark 1:16-20; Luke 5:1-11.
5. Alan Hirsh, *The Forgotten Ways: Reactivating the Missional Church* (Grand Rapids, MI: Brazos Press, 2006), Chapter 4 "Disciple Making" under the section "The Conspiracy of 'Little Jesus,'" Kindle.

Session 8: Teach

1. The three-thirds process originated with Ying and Grace Kai and is discussed at length by Steve Smith in "The Three-Thirds Process," *T4T: A Discipleship ReRevolution* (Monument, CO: WIGTake Resources, 2011).
2. The intentional process of raising believers to lead in disciple making on their own as described in this paragraph is often described by the acronym MAWL which stands for Model, Assist, Watch, and Leave (or Letter).
3. Mark Dever, *The Church: The Gospel Made Visible* (Nashville, TN: B&H Publishing Group, 2012). Though my list is not entirely the same as the characteristics that Mark Dever discusses, this book was the primary source that I used to check my list of healthy church characteristics.
4. This view has been supported by the record of Jesus rising from the dead and appearing to His disciples on Sunday, as well as Paul meeting with a group in Troas on the first day of the week (Acts 20:7) and asking the church in Corinth to make a collection for the Christians in Jerusalem on the first day of every week (1 Corinthians 16:1-2). Paul writes in Romans,

"One person esteems one day as better than another, while another esteems all days alike. Each one should be fully convinced in his own mind. The one who observes the day, observes it in honor of the Lord. The one who eats, eats in honor of the Lord, since he gives thanks to God, while the one who abstains, abstains in honor of the Lord and gives thanks to God" (Romans 14:5-6).

5. IMB has adopted the following definition and guidelines for church.

Church Definition (*Baptist Faith and Message 2000*, Southern Baptist Convention): "A New Testament church of the Lord Jesus Christ is an autonomous local congregation of baptized believers, associated by covenant in the faith and fellowship of the gospel; observing the two ordinances of Christ, governed by His laws, exercising the gifts, rights, and privileges invested in them by His Word, and seeking to extend the gospel to the ends of the earth. Each congregation operates under the Lordship of Christ through democratic processes. In such a congregation each member is responsible and accountable to Christ as Lord. Its scriptural officers are pastors and deacons. While both men and women are gifted for service in the church, the office of pastor is limited to men as qualified by Scripture.

The New Testament speaks also of the church as the Body of Christ which includes all of the redeemed of all the ages, believers from every tribe, and tongue, and people, and nation."

Church Guidelines (approved by IMB trustees, January 2005): We believe that every local church is autonomous under the Lordship of Jesus Christ and the authority of His inerrant word. This is as true overseas as it is in the United States, and some churches to which we relate overseas may make decisions in doctrine and practice which we would not have chosen. Nevertheless, we are accountable to God and to Southern Baptists for the foundation that we lay when we plant churches, for the teaching that we give when we train church leaders, and for the criteria that we use when we count churches. In our church planting and teaching ministries, we will seek to lay a foundation of beliefs and practices that are consistent with the *Baptist Faith and Message 2000*, although local churches overseas may express those beliefs and practices in different ways according to the needs of their cultural settings. Flowing from the definition of a church given above and from the Scriptures from which this definition is derived, we will observe the following guidelines in church planting, leadership training and statistical reporting.

- A church is intentional about being a church. The members think of themselves as a church and they are committed to one another and to God (associated by covenant) in pursuing all that Scripture requires of a church.
- A church has an identifiable membership of baptized believers in Jesus Christ.
- A church practices the baptism of believers only by immersing them in water.
- A church observes the Lord's Supper on a regular basis.
- Under the authority of the local church and its leadership, members may be assigned to carry out the ordinances.
- A church submits to the inerrant Word of God as the ultimate authority for all that it believes and does.

- A church meets regularly for worship, prayer, the study of God's Word, and fellowship. Members of the church minister to one another's needs, hold each other accountable, and exercise church discipline as needed. They encourage one another and build each other up in holiness, maturity in Christ, and love.
- A church embraces their responsibility to fulfill the Great Commission, both locally and globally, from the beginning of their existence as a church.
- A church is autonomous and self-governing under the Lordship of Jesus Christ and the authority of His Word.
- A church has identifiable leaders, who are scrutinized and set apart according to the qualifications set forth in Scripture. They recognize two biblical offices of church leadership: pastors/elders/overseers and deacons. While both men and women are gifted for service in the church, the office of pastor/elder/overseer is limited to men as qualified by Scripture.

6. For further information on healthy churches, I suggest the many resources available through 9Marks, http://www.9marks.org/.
7. Bob Roberts Jr., *Transformation: How Glocal Churches Transform Lives and the World* (Grand Rapids, MI: Zondervan, 2006), 15, Kindle.

Session 9: Reach

1. Names changed in this story to protect the identity of those individuals.
2. The study on how Jesus chose leaders was influenced by Wilson Geisler, "Jesus' Method for Leadership Multiplication and Development," "Rapidly Advancing Disciples (RAD): A Practical Implementation of Current Best Practices (2011)," 4, Accessed November 14, 2012, http://www.churchplantingmovements.com/.
3. Dave Ferguson and Alan Hirsh, *On the Verge: A Journey into the Apostolic Future of the Church*, EPub Edition (Grand Rapids, MI: Zondervan, 2011), End of "Introduction," Kindle.

ACKNOWLEDGMENTS

There are a number of leaders and pastors, past and present, whose books and messages have certainly influenced me and, therefore, this material—they have all been referenced in the Endnotes or Recommended Resources.

I'm indebted to my mentor, Calvin Taylor, a veteran missionary who poured wisdom and experience into my life that I continue to draw from on a daily basis.

There are many cross-cultural workers and nationals that my wife and I have lived and worked alongside overseas that we'd like to thank but must remain nameless for security reasons—these friends are like family to us and have shaped many aspects of who we are. I'd like to give a special thanks to Jacob Franklin who provided the opportunity to pilot this study and encouraged me throughout the writing process. I'd like to thank those who have been a huge support in this project, including Chuck Lawless, Mike Lopez and Caleb Crider. Thanks to Chad Stillwell for recommending this small-group version.

My wife and I would like to thank our parents and siblings who have supported and encouraged us in everything we've set after and through every challenge we've faced.

Thanks to our sweet little daughter and cute little boy who light up every day—you are both such blessings and we love you so much!

I'd like to thank my beautiful and creative wife—my ministry partner and best friend. We've lived, processed, and sought the Lord through all of this together. She has had a very active role throughout the journaling, studying, researching, writing, rewriting, and editing of this study.

Above all, I praise God for rescuing me and inviting me to be a part of His work. I am so grateful that, in His love, He gave us His Word that we might know Him and His will for our lives. He has given us all we need for life and godliness (2 Peter 1:3-11).

GLOSSARY

abide *v.* remain connected and committed to Jesus

baptism *n.* the act of immersing believers in water as an obedient symbol of their faith

believer *n.* a person rescued by and following Jesus as their Lord and Savior

bridge 1) *v.* to transition the topic of conversation to the gospel, 2) *n.* the topic by which you change conversation to the gospel

Christian *n.* SEE believer

church planting *n.* the work of evangelism, discipleship, and raising leaders for the establishment of a reproducing local church

community *n.* a group of people bonded together with a common identity and purpose

connect *v.* personally know and be engaged in people's lives

disciple 1) *n.* a devoted follower, 2) *v.* instruct a devoted follower

discipleship *n.* equipping, modeling, and holding followers of Jesus accountable, SEE also equip

entry points *n.* the places where you meet people and make inroads into their community

equip *v.* instruct believers in knowing and obeying the Word

expect *v.* have confidence that the Spirit will guide you and convict the lost

evangelize *v.* make the gospel known and invite a response

faith *n.* 1) trust in Jesus, 2) a conviction that something is true

far-culture *adj.* from a distant people group, in language and/or culture, to the target people group

Father *n. prop.* God

go *v.* take the gospel to the lost

gospel *n.* the good news of Jesus

gospel-centered *adj.* everything focused on Jesus and what He did

gospel-centered life *n.* your life totally focused on knowing and praising Jesus

gospel-centered mission *n.* your work totally focused on making Jesus known and praised

heart language *n.* the first or primary language spoken by a person or people group

high view *n.* very high opinion and priority

His story SEE gospel

holy *adj.* perfect and pure, set apart

identify *v.* work to understand people's lives, needs, and how to advance the gospel among them

journey *n.* your personal story of knowing and following Jesus

lead *v.* raise up leaders so that churches can stand on their own and continue the mission of making disciples

long-term discipleship *n.* mentorship and on-going study of growing in and obeying the Word

Lord's Supper *n.* the act of obediently remembering Jesus' death and anticipating His return through sharing of the bread and the fruit of the vine

lost *n.* persons who are not followers of Jesus

love *v.* genuinely express interest, care, and honor

mission *n.* the work of making disciples

model *v.* 1) be an example of Jesus, 2) show in action how to live a godly life and be on mission for Jesus

mother tongue *n.* SEE heart language

multiply *v.* disciples of Jesus grow in godliness and reproduce themselves by making disciples of Jesus

my story *n.* your personal story of your life before you met Jesus, how you met Jesus, and your life since being rescued by Jesus and making Him the Lord of your life

near-culture *adj.* from a different but similar people group, in language and/or culture, to the target people group

obedience-based discipleship *n.* active growth in both knowledge of and obedience to Jesus, typically in accountability with believers

obey *v.* follow the teaching of God's Word and guidance of the Spirit

one *adj.* having an unbroken and undivided commonality and purpose in something (e.g. in community)

one thing *n.* a single, intent focus and priority

people group *n.* a group of people who share a common language, culture and/or identity

preach *v.* provide an opportunity for the lost to hear the gospel, SEE evangelize

reach *v.* geographically saturate ethno-linguistic tribes with the gospel in an effort to make disciples who make disciples and churches that plant churches

rescued *adj.* undeservingly freed by Jesus from the consequences of sin

same-culture *adj.* from the target people group

saved *adj.* SEE rescued

seed *n.* the gospel

seeker *n.* a lost person who is receptive to the gospel

share *v.* SEE evangelize

short-term discipleship *n.* the mentorship and topical studies that 1) lay foundations for new believers; or 2) encourage specific areas of growth in existing believers.

sifting *n.* a difficult experience that the Spirit intends to use for good

sin *n.* the imperfections all people have that, apart from Jesus, separate them from God

sow *v.* share the gospel, SEE evangelize

surrender *v.* give up all of yourself

teach *v.* instruct believers in how to grow in godliness and make disciples

training *n.* a time of specialized teaching or instruction for believers

tribe *n.* 1) SEE people group, 2) an identity or bond with a group(s) of people that is based around common interests and may supersede their identification with their ethno-linguistic group

vision *n.* something seen or understood in faith

vision-casting 1) *n.* sharing a vision of an increasing number of lost people knowing and worshipping Jesus 2) *n.* inviting and empowering believers to be involved in taking the gospel to the lost

Word *n.* the Bible